Feb. 1942.

Leeds.

THE NEW TEMPLE SHAKESPEARE

Edited by M. R. Ridley, M.A.

MACBETH

by William Shakespeare

London: J. M. DENT & SONS LTD.
New York: E. P. DUTTON & CO. INC.

All rights reserved
Printed in Great Britain
by Turnbull & Spears at Edinburgh
and decorated by

Eric Gill

for

J. M. Dent & Sons Ltd.

Aldine House Bedford St. London
Toronto . *Vancouver*
Melbourne . *Wellington*
First Published in this edition 1935

Editor's General Note

The Text. The editor has kept before him the aim of presenting to the modern reader the nearest possible approximation to what Shakespeare actually wrote. The text is therefore conservative, and is based on the earliest reliable printed text. But to avoid distraction (*a*) the spelling is modernised, and (*b*) a limited number of universally accepted emendations is admitted without comment. Where a Quarto text exists as well as the First Folio the passages which occur only in the Quarto are enclosed in square brackets [ ] and those which occur only in the Folio in brace brackets { }.

Scene Division. The rapid continuity of the Elizabethan curtainless production is lost by the 'traditional' scene divisions. Where there is an essential difference of place these scene divisions are retained. Where on the other hand the change of place is insignificant the scene division is indicated only by a space on the page. For ease of reference, however, the 'traditional' division is retained at the head of the page and in line numbering.

Notes. Passages on which there are notes are indicated by a † in the margin.

Punctuation adheres more closely than has been usual to the 'Elizabethan' punctuation of the early texts. It is often therefore more indicative of the way in which the lines were to be delivered than of their syntactical construction.

Glossaries are arranged on a somewhat novel principle, not alphabetically, but in the order in which the words or phrases occur. The editor is much indebted to Mr J. N. Bryson for his collaboration in the preparation of the glossaries.

Preface

The Text. The only text for the play is that of the First Folio. The MS. from which it was set, whether original or transcript, was almost certainly a prompt copy, since the stage directions are rather unusually full, and at one point (II. iii. 80) what was presumably the prompter's note for himself, *Ring the bell*, seems to have crept from the stage-directions into the text; and probably a copy that had been cut for stage presentation, since the play is abnormally short (the shortest of all except *The Comedy of Errors*), and exhibits a number of awkwardnesses where it looks as though the ragged edges of the cuts had not been joined. (As against this it should be pointed out that the Malcolm-Macduff scene in England, all but about fifteen lines of which is of small dramatic value and is little more than a versification of Holinshed, stands in all its interminable length.) In particular all readers must feel that the greater part of the last Act, apart from a few deservedly famous passages, is huddled and muddled, and it contains in F one piece of confusion in important stage business which is tidied out of modern editions. As to whether the copy was an original or a transcript the data seem to me inadequate for more than very conjectural determination. The number of certainly or probably corrupt passages suggests that the compositor, unless he was careless and incompetent, had not at any rate in front of him the work of an expert scrivener (unless indeed the poor scrivener had difficulty with *his* copy). But the compositor, at least in the more mechanical details of his job, was far from careless and incompetent. There are comparatively few of the ordinary minor errors, such as transposed and turned letters; he is rather unusually careful about the apostrophe in the *'d* terminations; and the punctuation is elaborate, if not excessive. One's guess would be, I think, that the copy was the original MS., cut for the stage, and used as the prompt book, were it not that if the original had been extant one would have expected some of the stage-cuts to be restored for what was a reading edition; and the most probable conjecture is perhaps that we are reading a not very skilful transcript of the cut original, a transcript which had been used as the prompt book and had perhaps also incorporated some additional matter, *e.g.* the Hecate passages (of which more later).

Date of Composition. The accepted date is 1605-6, though that date is arrived at by different commentators by different roads, and I do not know that any detailed examination of the evidence is of much profit. I think indeed that any reader who will examine the data as admirably and cautiously marshalled by Sir Edmund Chambers in his *William Shakespeare* will conceive a most healthy distrust of 'allusion' evidence. To take only one instance, the famous 'equivocator' is pretty clearly connected with the trial of Garnet in March 1606. But he has no articulated relevance in the Porter's speech, and could very easily have been a later insertion for the sake of an effective topical hit.

Possible Interpolations. Almost no critic has been satisfied to suppose that the whole play as we have it is Shakespeare's. Even a very conservative judgment would excise three passages (III. v., IV. i. 39-43, 125-32) in the witch-scenes, " which can be distinguished from the genuine text by the introduction of Hecate, by the use of an iambic instead of a trochaic metre, and by prettiness of lyrical fancy alien to the main conception of the witches." It is to be noticed that the two songs indicated by their opening words at III. v. 35 and IV. i. 43 are given in full in Thomas Middleton's *The Witch*, and he may well have been the interpolator, if interpolator there was. But why any company should go to the trouble (unless Hecate had some topical theatrical value of which we know nothing) of having the interpolations made, the one unnecessary and the other two both unnecessary and trivial, has not been adequately explained. The more self-confident and swashbuckling critics, beginning with Coleridge, have been much more drastic, and have unloaded on to an unhappy but hypothetical interpolator all the passages which they regarded as 'un-Shakespearean.' All the witch-scenes, the Porter-scene, much of the fighting in Act V., as well as some isolated fragments, have all fallen under the ban of some critic or other. But the making of these excisions, and others like them in other plays, is based upon an implicit claim made by the critic, a claim the arrogance of which is only concealed because it is not explicitly stated, that he can distinguish not only between Shakespeare's work *at his best* and that of inferior craftsmen (that is a distinction which anyone with an ear can draw) but between Shakespeare doing hurried journeyman's work and other journeymen. Every reader who has any sense of style must find himself in reading the play being often arrested and sometimes shocked by startling incongruities. It is no doubt extremely odd to find Macbeth, in the last few lines of III. iv., after a thoroughly characteristic 'late' Shakespearean passage with Lady Macbeth, suddenly suffering from a spasm of couplets; and it is even odder to find V. v. opening at least adequately, rising to the great 'To-morrow, and to-morrow, and to-morrow' speech, and then tailing off into poorish stuff and ending with three of the feeblest couplets that even Shakespeare ever perpetrated. I think that if one is to read the play with intelligence one's ear should be alert to these oddities; but they are not 'evidence' of anything except that the play exhibits the most disconcerting shifts from one stylistic plane to another. They suggest interesting possibilities, and that is all. For what little a personal opinion is worth, and in such questions that is very little, most of the disputed passages, even including those of Hecate but excluding the bulk of the witch-scenes (and paying no attention to Coleridge's refined distaste for the Porter), do not strike on my ear so much as 'non-Shakespeare' but rather as 'non-*Macbeth*.' I do not, that is, find it at all hard to believe that Shakespeare wrote them, but very hard to believe that he wrote them at the same time as most of the rest of the play. Shakespeare is often unequal, but seldom in this way. He can write poor stuff even in his later plays, but it is poor stuff in his later manner and not in his earlier. It is a tempting speculation that Shakespeare may possibly, at the time when he was using Holinshed so largely for his English Histories, have roughed out a play of Macbeth with more stress upon the historical side of it, a play in which the Malcolm-Macduff scene in England and the excursions and alarums of the last Act would be much more in place than in the tragedy which we now have. But that is no more than idle speculation; it might account for some of the peculiarities of the play, but there is not a shred of evidence to support it, and I have certainly not the hardihood to advance it even as a 'conjecture.'

Sources. Apart from the demonological details, for which, if we demand a printed source rather than verbal tradition, we can suppose Shakespeare indebted to Scot's *Discoverie of Witchcraft* (1584), the undoubted source is Holinshed's *Chronicle of England and Scotland*, probably in the second (1587) edition. The whole of the main story is there, including the witches, and so are many of even the minor details. Of all the plays in which Shakespeare used Holinshed this provides the most fascinating study of the way in which Shakespeare transmuted his sources, a study comparable in interest to a study of the way in which he used North's *Plutarch*, but the parallelism is so continuous that to exhibit it in full would occupy disproportionate space, and a few instances must suffice. Here are two small details: in Holinshed " he (Makdowald) had gotten togither a mightie power of men: for *out of the westerne Iles* there came unto him a great multitude of people, offering to assist him in that rebellious quarell, and out of Ireland in hope of the spoile came no small number of *Kernes and Galloglasses*." In *Macbeth*, I. ii. 9-13:

> *The merciless Macdonwald*
> *. . . . . . from the western isles*
> *Of kerns and gallowglasses is supplied.*

In Holinshed, after Duff's murder, portents are recorded. "Monstrous sights also that were seene within the Scotish kingdome that yeere were these: horsses in Louthian, being of singular beautie and swiftnesse, did eate their owne flesh, and would in no wise taste anie other meate. . . . There was a sparhawke also strangled by an owle. Neither was it anie lesse woonder that the sunne, as before is said, was continuallie covered with clouds for six moneths space." In *Macbeth* II. iv. seems to be there for little other purpose than to present a vivid versification of Holinshed. And here is Holinshed on the witches:

Shortlie after happened a strange and vncouth woonder, which afterward was the cause of much trouble in the realme of Scotland, as ye shall after heare. It fortuned as Makbeth and Banquho iournied towards Fores, where the king then laie, they went sporting by the waie togither without other companie, saue onelie themselues, passing thorough the woods and fields, when suddenlie in the middest of a laund, there met them three women in strange and wild apparell, resembling creatures of elder world, whome when they attentiuelie beheld, woondering much at the sight, the first of them spake and said: " All haile, Makbeth, thane of Glammis ! " (for he had latelie entered into that dignitie and office by the death of his father Sinell). The second of them said: " Haile, Makbeth, thane of Cawder ! " But the third said: " All haile, Makbeth, that heereafter shalt be king of Scotland ! "

Then Banquho: " What manner of women " (saith he) " are you, that seeme so little fauourable vnto me, whereas to my fellow heere, besides high offices, ye assigne also the kingdome, appointing foorth nothing for me at all ? " " Yes " (saith the first of them), " we promise greater benefits vnto thee, than vnto him, for he shall reigne in deed, but with an vnluckie end: neither shall he leaue anie issue behind him to succeed in his place, where contrarilie thou in deed shalt not reigne at all, but of thee those shall be borne which shall gouerne the Scotish kingdome by long order of continuall descent." Herewith the foresaid women vanished immediatlie out of their sight. This was reputed at the first but some vaine fantasticall illusion by Mackbeth and Banquho, insomuch that Banquho would call Mackbeth in iest, king of Scotland; and Mackbeth againe would call him in sport likewise, the father of manie kings. But afterwards the common opinion was, that these women were either the weird sisters, that is (as ye would say) the goddesses of destinie, or else some nymphs or feiries, indued with knowledge of prophesie by their necromanticall science, bicause euerie thing came to passe as they had spoken. For shortlie after the thane of Cawder being condemned at Fores of treason against the king committed; his lands, liuings, and offices were giuen of the kings liberalitie to Mackbeth.

The same night after, at supper, Banquho iested with him and said: "Now Mackbeth thou hast obteined those things which the two former sisters prophesied, there remaineth onelie for thee to purchase that which the third said should come to passe." Wherevpon Mackbeth reuoluing the thing in his mind, began euen then to deuise how he might atteine to the kingdome: but yet he thought with himselfe that he must tarie a time, which should aduance him thereto (by the diuine prouidence) as it had come to passe in his former preferment. But shortlie after it chanced that king Duncane, hauing two sonnes by his wife which was the daughter of Siward earle of Northumberland, he made the elder of them, called Malcolme, prince of Cumberland, as it were thereby to appoint him his successor in the kingdome, immediatlie after his deceasse. Mackbeth sore troubled herewith, for that he saw by this means his hope sore hindered (where, by the old lawes of the realme, the ordinance was, that if he that should succeed were not of able age to take the charge vpon himselfe, he that was next of blood vnto him should be admitted), he began to take counsell how he might vsurpe the kingdome by force, hauing a iust quarell so to doo (as he tooke the matter) for that Duncane did what in him lay to defraud him of all manner of title and claime, which he might in time to come, pretend vnto the crowne.

Duration of Action. I. i.-iii. will go well enough into one day, though the timing of these preliminary scenes is of small importance. From I. iv. to the end of II. occupies about twenty-four hours, from the morning of one day to the morning of the next. There is then an interval of uncertain length; Macbeth is King and Banquo's suspicions are growing. III. i.-iv. occupy something less than twenty-four hours, from the late morning of one day to the very early morning of the next. III. v. and vi. are 'timeless,' and IV. i. completes the previous twenty-four hours. IV. ii. we can fit into the same period or not as we choose. There is then an interval for Ross's journey to England, followed by IV. iii. There is then an interval for the gathering of the hostile forces. Act V. occupies from the night of one day to some time on the next day, though we can with Daniel introduce intervals into this Act if we feel them necessary. It is noticeable, and characteristic of the atmosphere of the play, that the main 'days' of the action are not days, but nights.

Criticism.

Hazlitt.[1]—Macbeth (generally speaking) is done upon a stronger and more systematic principle of contrast than any other of Shakespear's plays. It moves upon the verge of an abyss, and is a constant struggle between life and death. The action is desperate and the reaction is dreadful. It is a huddling together of fierce extremes, a war of opposite natures which of them shall destroy the other. There is nothing but what has a violent end or violent beginnings. The lights and shades are laid on with a determined hand; the transitions from triumph to despair, from the height of terror to the repose of death, are sudden and startling; every passion brings in its fellow-contrary, and the thoughts pitch and jostle against each other as in the dark. The whole play is an

---

[1] *The Characters of Shakespear's Plays.*

unruly chaos of strange and forbidden things, where the ground rocks under our feet. Shakespear's genius here took its full swing, and trod upon the farthest bounds of nature and passion. This circumstance will account for the abruptness and violent antitheses of the style, the throes and labour which run through the expression, and from defects will turn them into beauties.

De Quincey.[1]—From my boyish days I had always felt a great perplexity on one point in *Macbeth*. It was this: The knocking at the gate which succeeds to the murder of Duncan produced to my feelings an effect for which I never could account. The effect was that it reflected back upon the murderer a peculiar awfulness and a depth of solemnity; yet, however obstinately I endeavoured with my understanding to comprehend this, for many years I never could see *why* it should produce such an effect.

.   .   .   .

At length I solved it to my own satisfaction; and my solution is this:—Murder, in ordinary cases, where the sympathy is wholly directed to the case of the murdered person, is an incident of coarse and vulgar horror; and for this reason,—that it flings the interest exclusively upon the natural but ignoble instinct by which we cleave to life: an instinct which, as being indispensable to the primal law of self-preservation, is the same in kind (though different in degree) amongst all living creatures. This instinct, therefore, because it annihilates all distinctions, and degrades the greatest of men to the level of " the poor beetle that we tread on," exhibits human nature in its most abject and humiliating attitude. Such an

---

[1] *On the Knocking on the Gate in Macbeth.*

attitude would little suit the purposes of the poet. What then must he do? He must throw the interest on the murderer. Our sympathy must be with *him* (of course I mean a sympathy of comprehension, a sympathy by which we enter into his feelings, and are made to understand them,—not a sympathy of pity or approbation). In the murdered person, all strife of thought, all flux and reflux of passion and of purpose, are crushed by one overwhelming panic; the fear of instant death smites him " with its petrific mace." But in the murderer, such a murderer as a poet will condescend to, there must be raging some great storm of passion,—jealousy, ambition, vengeance, hatred,—which will create a hell within him; and into this hell we are to look.

In *Macbeth*, for the sake of gratifying his own enormous and teeming faculty of creation, Shakspere has introduced two murderers: and, as usual in his hands, they are remarkably discriminated: but,—though in Macbeth the strife of mind is greater than in his wife, the tiger spirit not so awake, and his feelings caught chiefly by contagion from her,—yet, as both were finally involved in the guilt of murder, the murderous mind of necessity is finally to be presumed in both. This was to be expressed; and, on its own account, as well as to make it a more proportionable antagonist to the unoffending nature of their victim, " the gracious Duncan," and adequately to expound " the deep damnation of his taking off," this was to be expressed with peculiar energy. We were to be made to feel that the human nature,—*i.e.* the divine nature of love and mercy, spread through the hearts of all creatures, and seldom utterly withdrawn from man,—was gone, vanished, extinct, and that the fiendish nature had taken its place. And, as this effect is marvellously accomplished in the *dialogues* and *soliloquies* themselves, so it is finally consummated by the expedient under consideration; and it is to this that I now solicit the reader's attention. If the reader has ever witnessed a wife, daughter, or sister in a fainting fit, he may chance to have observed that the most affecting moment in such a spectacle is *that* in which a sigh and a stirring announce the recommencement of suspended life. Or, if the reader has ever been present in a vast metropolis on the day when some great national idol was carried in funeral pomp to his grave, and, chancing to walk near the course through which it passed, has felt powerfully, in the silence and desertion of the streets, and in the stagnation of ordinary business, the deep interest which at that moment was possessing the heart of man,—if all at once he should hear the death-like stillness broken up by the sound of wheels rattling away from the scene, and making known that the transitory vision was dissolved, he will be aware that at no moment was his sense of the complete suspension and pause in ordinary human concerns so full and affecting as at that moment when the suspension ceases, and the goings-on of human life are suddenly resumed. All action in any direction is best expounded, measured, and made apprehensible, by reaction. Now, apply this to the case in *Macbeth*. Here, as I have said, the retiring of the human heart and the entrance of the fiendish heart was to be expressed and made sensible. Another world has stept in; and the murderers are taken out of the region of human things, human purposes, human desires. They are transfigured: Lady Macbeth is " unsexed "; Macbeth has forgot that he was born of woman; both are conformed to the image of devils; and the world of devils is suddenly revealed. But how shall this be conveyed and made palpable? In order that a new world may step in, this world must for a time disappear. The murderers and the murder must be insulated—cut off by an immeasurable gulf from the ordinary tide and succession of human affairs—locked up and sequestered in some deep recess; we must be made sensible that the world of ordinary life is suddenly arrested, laid asleep, tranced, racked into a dread armistice; time must be annihilated, relation to things without abolished; and all must pass self-withdrawn into a deep syncope and suspension of earthly passion. Hence it is that, when the deed is done, when the work of darkness is perfect, then the world of darkness passes away like a pageantry in the clouds: the knocking at the gate is heard, and it makes known audibly that the reaction has commenced; the human has made its reflux upon the fiendish; the pulses of life are beginning to beat again; and the re-establishment of the goings-on of the world in which we live first makes us profoundly sensible of the awful parenthesis that had suspended them.

O mighty poet! Thy works are not as those of other men, simply and merely great works of art, but are also like the phenomena of nature, like the sun and the sea, the stars and the flowers, like frost and snow, rain and dew, hail-storm and thunder, which are to be studied with entire submission of our own faculties, and in the perfect faith that in them there can be no too much or too little, nothing useless or inert, but that, the farther we press in our discoveries, the more we shall see proofs of design and self-supporting arrangement where the careless eye had seen nothing but accident!

Bradley.—The special popularity of *Hamlet* and *Macbeth* is due in part to some of these common characteristics, notably to the fascination of the supernatural, the absence of the spectacle of extreme undeserved suffering, the absence of characters which horrify and repel and yet are destitute of grandeur. The reader who looks unwillingly at Iago gazes at Lady Macbeth in awe, because though she is dreadful she is also sublime. The whole tragedy is sublime.

In this, however, and in other respects, *Macbeth* makes an impression quite different from that of *Hamlet*. The dimensions of the principal characters, the rate of movement in the action, the supernatural effect, the style, the versification, are all changed; and they are all changed in much the same manner. In many parts of *Macbeth* there is in the language a peculiar compression, pregnancy, energy, even violence; the harmonious grace and even flow, often conspicuous in *Hamlet*, have almost disappeared. The chief characters, built on a scale at least as large as that of *Othello*, seem to attain at times an almost superhuman stature. The diction has in places a huge and rugged grandeur, which degenerates here and there into tumidity. The solemn majesty of the royal Ghost in *Hamlet*, appearing in armour and standing silent in the moonlight, is exchanged for shapes of horror, dimly seen in the murky air or revealed by the glare of the caldron fire in a dark cavern, or for the ghastly face of Banquo badged with blood and staring with blank eyes. The other three tragedies all open with conversations which lead into the action: here the action bursts into wild life amidst the sounds of a thunderstorm and the echoes of a distant battle. It hurries through seven very brief scenes of mounting suspense to a terrible crisis, which is reached, in the murder of Duncan, at the beginning of the Second Act. Pausing a moment and changing its shape, it hastes again with scarcely diminished speed to fresh horrors. And even when the speed of the outward action is slackened, the same effect is continued in another form: we are shown a soul tortured by an agony which admits not a moment's repose, and rushing in frenzy towards its doom. *Macbeth* is very much shorter than the other three tragedies, but our experience in traversing it is so crowded and intense that it leaves an impression not of brevity but of speed. It is the most vehement, the most concentrated, perhaps we may say the most tremendous, of the tragedies.

A Shakespearean tragedy, as a rule, has a special tone or atmosphere of its own, quite perceptible, however difficult to describe. The effect of this atmosphere is marked with unusual strength in *Macbeth*. It is due to a variety of influences which combine with those just noticed, so that, acting and reacting, they form a whole; and the desolation of the blasted heath, the design of the Witches, the guilt in the hero's soul, the darkness of the night, seem to emanate from one and the same source. This effect is strengthened by a multitude of small touches, which at the moment may be little noticed but still leave their mark on the imagination. We may approach the consideration of the characters and the action by distinguishing some of the ingredients of this general effect.

Darkness, we may even say blackness, broods over this tragedy. It is remarkable that almost all the scenes which at once recur to memory take place either at night or in some dark spot. The vision of the dagger, the murder of Duncan, the murder of Banquo, the sleep-walking of Lady Macbeth, all come in night-scenes. The Witches dance in the thick air of a storm, or, ' black and midnight hags,' receive Macbeth in a cavern. The blackness of night is to the hero a thing of fear, even of horror; and that which he feels becomes the spirit of the play. The faint glimmerings of the western sky at twilight are here menacing: it is the hour when the traveller hastens to reach safety in his inn, and when Banquo rides homeward to meet his assassins; the hour when ' light thickens,' when ' night's black agents to their prey do rouse,' when the wolf begins to howl, and the owl to scream, and withered murder steals forth to his work. Macbeth bids the stars hide their fires that his 'black' desires may be concealed; Lady Macbeth calls on thick night to come, palled in the dunnest smoke of hell. The moon is down and no stars shine when Banquo, dreading the dreams of the coming night, goes unwillingly to bed, and leaves Macbeth to wait for the summons of the little bell. When the next day should dawn, its light is 'strangled,' and 'darkness does the face of earth entomb.' In the whole drama the sun seems to shine only twice: first, in the beautiful but ironical passage where Duncan sees the swallows flitting round the castle of death; and, afterwards, when at the close the avenging army gathers to rid the earth of its shame. Of the many slighter touches which deepen this effect I notice only one. The failure of nature in Lady Macbeth is marked by her fear of darkness; 'she has light by her continually.' And in the one phrase of fear that escapes her lips even in sleep, it is of the darkness of the place of torment that she speaks.

The atmosphere of *Macbeth*, however, is not that of unrelieved blackness. On the contrary, as compared with *King Lear* and its cold dim gloom, *Macbeth* leaves a decided impression of colour; it is really the impression of a black night broken by flashes of light and colour, sometimes vivid and even glaring. They are the lights and colours of the thunder-storm in the first scene; of the dagger hanging before Macbeth's eyes and glittering alone in the midnight air; of the torch borne by the servant when he and his lord come upon Banquo crossing the castle-court to his room; of the torch, again, which Fleance carried to light his father to death, and which was dashed out by one of the murderers; of the torches that flared in the hall on the face of the Ghost and the blanched cheeks of Macbeth; of the flames beneath the boiling caldron from which the apparitions in the cavern rose; of the taper which showed to the Doctor and Gentlewoman the wasted face and blank eyes of Lady Macbeth. And, above all, the colour is the colour of blood.[1]

[1] Reprinted from *Shakespearian Tragedy* by permission of the Publishers, Macmillan & Co., Ltd.

THE TRAGEDY OF MACBETH

DRAMATIS PERSONÆ

DUNCAN, *king of Scotland.*
MALCOLM, } *his sons.*
DONALBAIN, }
MACBETH, } *generals of the King's army.*
BANQUO, }
MACDUFF, }
LENNOX, }
ROSS, }
MENTEITH, } *noblemen of Scotland.*
ANGUS, }
CAITHNESS, }
FLEANCE, *son to Banquo.*
SIWARD, *earl of Northumberland, general of the English forces.*
Young SIWARD, *his son.*
SEYTON, *an officer attending on Macbeth.*
BOY, *son to Macduff.*
An English Doctor.
A Scotch Doctor.
A Sergeant.
A Porter.
An Old Man.

Lady MACBETH.
Lady MACDUFF.
Gentlewoman attending on Lady Macbeth.

HECATE.
Three Witches.
Apparitions.

Lords, Gentlemen, Officers, Soldiers, Murderers, Attendants,
and Messengers.

SCENE: *Scotland ; England.*

THE TRAGEDY OF
MACBETH

Act First

A desert place

Thunder and Lightning.   Enter three Witches

1. *W.* When shall we three meet again ?
    In thunder, lightning, or in rain ?
2. *W.* When the hurlyburly 's done,
    When the battle 's lost, and won.
3. *W.* That will be ere the set of sun.
1. *W.* Where the place ?
2. *W.*   Upon the heath.
3. *W.* There to meet with Macbeth.
1. *W.* I come, Graymalkin.
All. Paddock calls :—anon !
    Fair is foul, and foul is fair.   10
    Hover through the fog and filthy air.   *Exeunt*

1

SCENE II

A camp near Forres

Alarum within.   Enter Duncan, Malcolm, Donalbain,
Lennox, with Attendants, meeting a bleeding Sergeant

Dun. What bloody man is that ?   He can report,
    As seemeth by his plight, of the revolt
    The newest state.

Mal.   This is the sergeant
    Who like a good and hardy soldier fought
    'Gainst my captivity.   Hail, brave friend !
    Say to the king the knowledge of the broil,
    As thou didst leave it.

Ser.   Doubtful it stood,
    As two spent swimmers, that do cling together
    And choke their art.   The merciless Macdonwald
    (Worthy to be a rebel, for to that   10
    The multiplying villanies of nature
    Do swarm upon him) from the western isles
    Of kerns and gallowglasses is supplied ;
    And fortune, on his damned quarrel smiling,
    Show'd like a rebel's whore : but all 's too weak :
    For brave Macbeth (well he deserves that name)
    Disdaining fortune, with his brandish'd steel,

Which smok'd with bloody execution,
Like valour's minion, carv'd out his passage,
Till he fac'd the slave ;   20
Which ne'er shook hands, nor bade farewell to him, †
Till he unseam'd him from the nave to the chops,
And fix'd his head upon our battlements.

Dun. O valiant cousin, worthy gentleman !

Ser. As whence the sun 'gins his reflection
Shipwrecking storms and direful thunders break,
So from that spring, whence comfort seem'd to come,
Discomfort swells. Mark, king of Scotland, mark,
No sooner justice had, with valour arm'd,
Compell'd these skipping kerns to trust their heels, 30
But the Norweyan lord, surveying vantage,
With furbish'd arms, and new supplies of men,
Began a fresh assault.

Dun.   Dismay'd not this
Our captains, Macbeth and Banquo ?

Ser.   Yes,
As sparrows eagles ; or the hare the lion.
If I say sooth, I must report they were
As cannons overcharg'd with double cracks ;
So they doubly redoubled strokes upon the foe :
Except they meant to bathe in reeking wounds,
Or memorize another Golgotha,   40

3

        I cannot tell—

        But I am faint, my gashes cry for help.

Dun. So well thy words become thee as thy wounds ;

        They smack of honour both.   Go get him surgeons.

                      Exit Sergeant, attended

        Who comes here ?

              Enter Ross and Angus

Mal.   The worthy thane of Ross.

Len. What a haste looks through his eyes ! So should he look

        That seems to speak things strange.

Ross.   God save the king !

Dun. Whence cam'st thou, worthy thane ?

Ross.   From Fife, great king,

        Where the Norweyan banners flout the sky

        And fan our people cold.   50

        Norway himself with terrible numbers,

        Assisted by that most disloyal traitor,

        The thane of Cawdor, began a dismal conflict,

        Till that Bellona's bridegroom, lapp'd in proof,

        Confronted him with self-comparisons,

        Point against point, rebellious arm 'gainst arm,

        Curbing his lavish spirit : and, to conclude,

        The victory fell on us.

Dun.   Great happiness !

*Ross.*That now

Sweno, the Norways' king, craves composition ;   60
Nor would we deign him burial of his men,
Till he disbursed, at Saint Colme's inch
Ten thousand dollars, to our general use.

*Dun.*No more that thane of Cawdor shall deceive
Our bosom interest : go pronounce his present death,
And with his former title greet Macbeth.

*Ross.*I 'll see it done.

*Dun.*What he hath lost, noble Macbeth hath won.

Exeunt

SCENE III

The heath

Thunder.   Enter the three Witches

1.*W.*Where hast thou been, sister ?

2.*W.*Killing swine.

3.*W.*Sister, where thou ?

1.*W.*A sailor's wife had chestnuts in her lap,
And mounch'd, and mounch'd, and mounch'd.
' Give me,' quoth I :
' Aroint thee, witch ! ' the rump-fed ronyon cries.
Her husband 's to Aleppo gone, master o' the Tiger ;
But in a sieve I 'll thither sail,

5

And, like a rat without a tail,
I 'll do, I 'll do, and I 'll do.   10
2. *W*.I 'll give thee a wind.
1. *W*.Thou 'rt kind.
3. *W*.And I another.
1. *W*.I myself have all the other,
And the very ports they blow,   †
All the quarters that they know
I' the shipman's card.
I 'll drain him dry as hay :
Sleep shall neither night nor day
Hang upon his pent-house lid ;   20
He shall live a man forbid :
Weary se'nnights, nine times nine,
Shall he dwindle, peak, and pine :
Though his bark cannot be lost,
Yet it shall be tempest-tost.
Look what I have.
2. *W*.Show me, show me,
1. *W*.Here I have a pilot's thumb,
Wreck'd as homeward he did come.   *Drum within*
3. *W*.A drum, a drum !   30
Macbeth doth come.
All. The weird sisters, hand in hand   †
Posters of the sea and land,

Thus do go, about, about,
Thrice to thine, and thrice to mine,
And thrice again, to make up nine.
Peace, the charm 's wound up.

Enter Macbeth and Banquo

Mac. So foul and fair a day I have not seen.

Ban. How far is 't call'd to Forres ?   What are these
So wither'd, and so wild in their attire,   40
That look not like the inhabitants o' the earth,
And yet are on 't ?   Live you or are you aught
That man may question ?   You seem to understand me,
By each at once her choppy finger laying
Upon her skinny lips : you should be women,
And yet your beards forbid me to interpret
That you are so.

Mac.   Speak, if you can : what are you ?

1. W. All hail, Macbeth, hail to thee thane of Glamis !

2. W. All hail, Macbeth ! hail to thee thane of Cawdor !

3. W. All hail, Macbeth, that shalt be king hereafter !   50

Ban. Good sir, why do you start, and seem to fear
Things that do sound so fair ?   I' the name of truth,
Are ye fantastical, or that indeed
Which outwardly ye show ?   My noble partner
You greet with present grace, and great prediction
Of noble having, and of royal hope,

7

That he seems rapt withal : to me you speak not :
If you can look into the seeds of time,
And say which grain will grow, and which will not,
Speak then to me, who neither beg, nor fear   60
Your favours, nor your hate.

1.*W*.Hail !

2.*W*.Hail !

3.*W*.Hail !

1.*W*.Lesser than Macbeth, and greater.

2.*W*.Not so happy, yet much happier.

3.*W*.Thou shalt get kings, though thou be none :
So all hail, Macbeth, and Banquo !

1.*W*.Banquo, and Macbeth, all hail !

Mac.Stay, you imperfect speakers, tell me more :   70
By Sinel's death I know I am thane of Glamis,
But how, of Cawdor ? the thane of Cawdor lives
A prosperous gentleman ; and to be king,
Stands not within the prospect of belief,
No more than to be Cawdor.   Say from whence
You owe this strange intelligence, or why
Upon this blasted heath you stop our way
With such prophetic greeting ?   Speak, I charge you.
                                        Witches vanish

Ban. The earth hath bubbles, as the water has,
And these are of them : whither are they vanish'd ?   80

*Mac.*Into the air : and what seem'd corporal melted
    As breath into the wind.   Would they had stay'd !

Ban. Were such things here, as we do speak about ?
    Or have we eaten on the insane root,
    That takes the reason prisoner ?

*Mac.*Your children shall be kings.

Ban.   You shall be king.

*Mac.*And thane of Cawdor too : went it not so ?

Ban. To the selfsame tune, and words.   Who 's here ?

            Enter Ross and Angus

*Ross.*The king hath happily receiv'd, Macbeth,
    The news of thy success : and when he reads   90
    Thy personal venture in the rebels' fight,
    His wonders and his praises do contend,
    Which should be thine, or his : silenc'd with that,
    In viewing o'er the rest o' the selfsame day,
    He finds thee in the stout Norweyan ranks,
    Nothing afeard of what thyself didst make,
    Strange images of death.   As thick as hail   †
    Came post with post, and every one did bear
    Thy praises in his kingdom's great defence,
    And pour'd them down before him.

Ang.   We are sent   100
    To give thee from our royal master thanks,
    Only to herald thee into his sight,

            Not pay thee.

Ross. And for an earnest of a greater honour,
  He bade me, from him, call thee thane of Cawdor :
  In which addition, hail, most worthy thane,
  For it is thine.

Ban.   What, can the devil speak true ?

Mac. The thane of Cawdor lives : why do you dress me
  In borrow'd robes ?

Ang.   Who was the thane, lives yet,
  But under heavy judgement bears that life,   110
  Which he deserves to lose. Whether he was com-
   bin'd
  With those of Norway, or did line the rebel
  With hidden help and vantage, or that with both
  He labour'd in his country's wreck, I know not ;
  But treasons capital, confess'd, and prov'd,
  Have overthrown him.

Mac.   (*aside*) Glamis, and thane of Cawdor :
  The greatest is behind.—Thanks for your pains.—
  Do you not hope your children shall be kings,
  When those that gave the thane of Cawdor to me
  Promis'd no less to them ?

Ban.   That, trusted home, 120
  Might yet enkindle you unto the crown,
  Besides the thane of Cawdor. But 'tis strange :

And oftentimes, to win us to our harm,
The instruments of darkness tell us truths,
Win us with honest trifles, to betray 's
In deepest consequence.
          Cousins, a word, I pray you.

Mac.   (*aside*) Two truths are told,
As happy prologues to the swelling act
Of the imperial theme.—I thank you, gentlemen.—
(*aside*) This supernatural soliciting   130
Cannot be ill ; cannot be good : if ill ?   †
Why hath it given me earnest of success,
Commencing in a truth ?   I am thane of Cawdor :
If good ? why do I yield to that suggestion,   †
Whose horrid image doth unfix my hair,
And make my seated heart knock at my ribs,
Against the use of nature ?   Present fears
Are less than horrible imaginings :
My thought, whose murder yet is but fantastical,
Shakes so my single state of man that function   140
Is smother'd in surmise, and nothing is,
But what is not.

Ban.   Look how our partner's rapt.

Mac. (*aside*) If chance will have me king, why, chance may
          crown me,
               Without my stir.

11

Ban.   New honours come upon him,
   Like our strange garments, cleave not to their mould,
   But with the aid of use.
Mac.   (*aside*) Come what come may,
   Time, and the hour, runs through the roughest day.
Ban. Worthy Macbeth, we stay upon your leisure.
Mac. Give me your favour : my dull brain was wrought
   With things forgotten.   Kind gentlemen, your pains   150
   Are register'd where every day I turn
   The leaf to read them.   Let us toward the king ;
   Think upon what hath chanc'd ; and at more time,
   The interim having weigh'd it, let us speak
   Our free hearts each to other.
Ban.   Very gladly.
Mac. Till then, enough.   Come, friends.   *Exeunt*

SCENE IV

Forres.   The palace

*Flourish.   Enter Duncan, Malcolm, Donalbain, Lennox,
   and Attendants*

Dun. Is execution done on Cawdor ?   Are not
   Those in commission yet return'd ?
Mal.   My liege,

They are not yet come back.   But I have spoke
With one that saw him die ; who did report
That very frankly he confess'd his treasons,
Implor'd your highness' pardon, and set forth
A deep repentance : nothing in his life
Became him like the leaving it ; he died
As one that had been studied in his death,
To throw away the dearest thing he ow'd   10
As 'twere a careless trifle.

Dun.   There 's no art
To find the mind's construction in the face :
He was a gentleman, on whom I built
An absolute trust.

       Enter Macbeth, Banquo, Ross, and Angus
           O worthiest cousin !
The sin of my ingratitude even now
Was heavy on me : thou art so far before,
That swiftest wing of recompense is slow,
To overtake thee.   Would thou hadst less deserv'd,
That the proportion both of thanks, and payment,
Might have been mine ! only I have left to say,   20
More is thy due than more than all can pay.

Mac. The service, and the loyalty I owe,
In doing it, pays itself.   Your highness' part
Is to receive our duties : and our duties

Are to your throne, and state, children, and servants ;
Which do but what they should, by doing every thing
Safe toward your love and honour.

Dun.   Welcome hither :
I have begun to plant thee, and will labour
To make thee full of growing.   Noble Banquo,
Thou hast no less deserv'd, nor must be known   30
No less to have done so : let me enfold thee,
And hold thee to my heart.

Ban.   There if I grow,
The harvest is your own.

Dun.   My plenteous joys,
Wanton in fulness, seek to hide themselves
In drops of sorrow.   Sons, kinsmen, thanes,
And you whose places are the nearest, know,
We will establish our estate upon
Our eldest, Malcolm, whom we name hereafter
The Prince of Cumberland : which honour must
Not unaccompanied invest him only,   40
But signs of nobleness, like stars, shall shine
On all deservers.   From hence to Inverness,
And bind us further to you.

Mac. The rest is labour, which is not us'd for you :   †
I 'll be myself the harbinger, and make joyful
The hearing of my wife with your approach ;

So humbly take my leave.

Dun.   My worthy Cawdor !

Mac.(*aside*) The Prince of Cumberland ! that is a step,
On which I must fall down, or else o'erleap,   50
For in my way it lies. Stars, hide your fires,
Let not light see my black and deep desires :
The eye wink at the hand ; yet let that be,
Which the eye fears, when it is done, to see.   *Exit*

Dun. True, worthy Banquo ; he is full so valiant,
And in his commendations I am fed ;
It is a banquet to me. Let 's after him,
Whose care is gone before, to bid us welcome :
It is a peerless kinsman.   *Flourish.   Exeunt*

SCENE V

Inverness.   Macbeth's castle

Enter Lady Macbeth, reading a letter

L.M.' They met me in the day of success ; and I have
learn'd by the perfect'st report, they have more in
them than mortal knowledge. When I burn'd in
desire to question them further, they made themselves air, into which they vanish'd. Whiles I stood
rapt in the wonder of it, came missives from the

king, who all-hail'd me Thane of Cawdor, by which
title, before, these weird sisters saluted me, and
referr'd me to the coming on of time, with " Hail,
king that shalt be ! "   This have I thought good to   10
deliver thee, my dearest partner of greatness, that
thou mightst not lose the dues of rejoicing by being
ignorant of what greatness is promis'd thee.   Lay it
to thy heart, and farewell.'
Glamis thou art, and Cawdor, and shalt be
What thou art promis'd : yet do I fear thy nature,
It is too full o' the milk of human kindness
To catch the nearest way.   Thou wouldst be great,
Art not without ambition, but without
The illness should attend it.   What thou wouldst
    highly,   20
That wouldst thou holily ; wouldst not play false,
And yet wouldst wrongly win.   Thou 'ldst have,
    great Glamis,
That which cries ' Thus thou must do, if thou have it ; '
And that which rather thou dost fear to do,
Than wishest should be undone.   Hie thee hither,
That I may pour my spirits in thine ear,
And chastise with the valour of my tongue
All that impedes thee from the golden round,
Which fate and metaphysical aid doth seem

To have thee crown'd withal.

Enter a Messenger

What is your tidings ?   30

Mes. The king comes here to-night.

L.M.   Thou 'rt mad to say it :

Is not thy master with him ? who, were 't so,
Would have inform'd for preparation.

Mes. So please you, it is true : our thane is coming :
One of my fellows had the speed of him,
Who, almost dead for breath, had scarcely more
Than would make up his message.

L.M.   Give him tending,

He brings great news,   *Exit Messenger*

the raven himself is hoarse
That croaks the fatal entrance of Duncan
Under my battlements.   Come, you spirits   40
That tend on mortal thoughts, unsex me here,
And fill me, from the crown to the toe, top-full
Of direst cruelty : make thick my blood,
Stop up the access and passage to remorse,
That no compunctious visitings of nature
Shake my fell purpose, nor keep peace between
The effect and it ! Come to my woman's breasts,
And take my milk for gall, you murdering ministers,
Wherever, in your sightless substances,

You wait on nature's mischief ! Come, thick night, 50
And pall thee in the dunnest smoke of hell,
That my keen knife see not the wound it makes,
Nor heaven peep through the blanket of the dark,
To cry ' Hold, hold ! '

Enter Macbeth

Great Glamis ! worthy Cawdor !
Greater than both, by the all-hail hereafter !
Thy letters have transported me beyond
This ignorant present, and I feel now
The future in the instant.

Mac.   My dearest love,
Duncan comes here to-night.

L.M.   And when goes hence ?

Mac. To-morrow, as he purposes.

L.M.   O, never   60
Shall sun that morrow see !
Your face, my thane, is as a book, where men
May read strange matters.   To beguile the time,
Look like the time, bear welcome in your eye,
Your hand, your tongue : look like the innocent flower,
But be the serpent under 't.   He that 's coming
Must be provided for : and you shall put
This night's great business into my dispatch,
Which shall to all our nights and days to come

18

      Give solely sovereign sway, and masterdom.   70

Mac. We will speak further.

L.M.   Only look up clear ;

      To alter favour ever is to fear :

      Leave all the rest to me.   *Exeunt*

SCENE VI

Before Macbeth's castle

Hautboys and torches.   Enter Duncan, Malcolm, Donalbain,
Banquo, Lennox, Macduff, Ross, Angus, and Attendants

Dun. This castle hath a pleasant seat, the air

      Nimbly and sweetly recommends itself

      Unto our gentle senses.

Ban.   This guest of summer,

      The temple-haunting martlet, does approve,

      By his loved mansionry, that the heaven's breath

      Smells wooingly here : no jutty, frieze,

      Buttress, nor coign of vantage, but this bird

      Hath made his pendant bed and procreant cradle :

      Where they most breed and haunt, I have observ'd

      The air is delicate.

Enter Lady Macbeth

Dun.   See, see, our honour'd hostess !   10

The love that follows us sometime is our trouble,
Which still we thank as love.   Herein I teach you
How you shall bid God 'ild us for your pains,
And thank us for your trouble.

L.M.   All our service,
In every point twice done, and then done double,
Were poor and single business, to contend
Against those honours deep and broad wherewith
Your majesty loads our house : for those of old,
And the late dignities heap'd up to them,
We rest your hermits.

Dun.   Where 's the thane of Cawdor ?   20
We cours'd him at the heels, and had a purpose
To be his purveyor : but he rides well,
And his great love, sharp as his spur, hath holp him
To his home before us.   Fair and noble hostess,
We are your guest to-night.

L.M.   Your servants ever
Have theirs, themselves, and what is theirs, in compt,
To make their audit at your highness' pleasure,
Still to return your own.

Dun.   Give me your hand ;
Conduct me to mine host : we love him highly,
And shall continue our graces towards him.   30
By your leave, hostess.   *Exeunt*

SCENE VII

Macbeth's castle

Hautboys and torches.   Enter a Sewer, and divers Servants
with dishes and service, and pass over the stage.   Then
enter Macbeth

Mac. If it were done, when 'tis done, then 'twere well
It were done quickly : if the assassination
Could trammel up the consequence, and catch,
With his surcease, success ; that but this blow
Might be the be-all and the end-all, here,
But here, upon this bank and shoal of time,
We 'ld jump the life to come.   But in these cases
We still have judgement here ; that we but teach
Bloody instructions, which being taught, return
To plague the inventor.   This even-handed justice   10
Commends the ingredients of our poison'd chalice
To our own lips.   He 's here in double trust ;
First, as I am his kinsman, and his subject,
Strong both against the deed ; then, as his host,
Who should against his murderer shut the door,
Not bear the knife myself.   Besides, this Duncan
Hath borne his faculties so meek, hath been
So clear in his great office, that his virtues

21

Will plead like angels, trumpet-tongu'd against
The deep damnation of his taking-off;   20
And pity, like a naked new-born babe,
Striding the blast, or heaven's cherubin, hors'd
Upon the sightless couriers of the air,
Shall blow the horrid deed in every eye,
That tears shall drown the wind.   I have no spur
To prick the sides of my intent, but only
Vaulting ambition, which o'erleaps itself,
And falls on the other.

Enter Lady Macbeth

How now? what news?

*L.M.*He has almost supp'd: why have you left the
chamber?

*Mac.*Hath he ask'd for me?

L.M.   Know you not he has?   30

*Mac.*We will proceed no further in this business:
He hath honour'd me of late, and I have bought
Golden opinions from all sorts of people,
Which would be worn now in their newest gloss,
Not cast aside so soon.

L.M.   Was the hope drunk,
Wherein you dress'd yourself? hath it slept since?
And wakes it now to look so green, and pale,
At what it did so freely?   From this time,

22

Such I account thy love. Art thou afeard
To be the same in thine own act and valour   40
As thou art in desire ? Wouldst thou have that
Which thou esteem'st the ornament of life,
And live a coward in thine own esteem ?
Letting ' I dare not ' wait upon ' I would,'
Like the poor cat i' the adage.   †

Mac.   Prithee peace :
I dare do all that may become a man,
Who dares do more, is none.

L.M.   What beast was 't then
That made you break this enterprize to me ?
When you durst do it, then you were a man ;
And, to be more than what you were, you would   50
Be so much more the man. Nor time, nor place,
Did then adhere, and yet you would make both :
They have made themselves, and that their fitness
        now
Does unmake you. I have given suck, and know
How tender 'tis to love the babe that milks me :
I would, while it was smiling in my face,
Have pluck'd my nipple from his boneless gums,
And dash'd the brains out, had I so sworn
As you have done to this.

Mac.   If we should fail ?

*L.M.*We fail ?   †
>But screw your courage to the sticking-place,   61
>And we 'll not fail : when Duncan is asleep,
>(Whereto the rather shall his day's hard journey
>Soundly invite him) his two chamberlains
>Will I with wine and wassail so convince,
>That memory, the warder of the brain,
>Shall be a fume, and the receipt of reason
>A limbec only : when in swinish sleep
>Their drenched natures lie as in a death,
>What cannot you and I perform upon   70
>The unguarded Duncan ? what not put upon
>His spongy officers, who shall bear the guilt
>Of our great quell ?

Mac.   Bring forth men-children only ;
>For thy undaunted mettle should compose
>Nothing but males.   Will it not be receiv'd,
>When we have mark'd with blood those sleepy
>   two
>Of his own chamber, and us'd their very daggers,
>That they have done 't ?

L.M.   Who dares receive it other,
>As we shall make our griefs and clamour roar
>Upon his death ?

Mac.   I am settled, and bend up   80

Each corporal agent to this terrible feat.
Away, and mock the time with fairest show :
False face must hide what the false heart doth know.

Exeunt

Act Second

Inverness.   Macbeth's castle

Enter Banquo, and Fleance bearing a torch before him

Ban. How goes the night, boy ?

Fle. The moon is down ; I have not heard the clock.

Ban. And she goes down at twelve.

Fle.   I take 't, 'tis later, sir.

Ban. Hold, take my sword : there 's husbandry in heaven,
       Their candles are all out : take thee that too.
       A heavy summons lies like lead upon me,
       And yet I would not sleep.   Merciful powers,
       Restrain in me the cursed thoughts that nature
       Gives way to in repose !

           Enter Macbeth, and a Servant with a torch

                          Give me my sword :

Who 's there ?   10

Mac. A friend.

Ban. What, sir, not yet at rest? The king 's a-bed :
He hath been in unusual pleasure, and
Sent forth great largess to your offices :
This diamond he greets your wife withal,
By the name of most kind hostess, and shut up
In measureless content.

Mac.   Being unprepar'd,
Our will became the servant to defect,
Which else should free have wrought.

Ban.   All 's well.
I dreamt last night of the three weird sisters :   20
To you they have show'd some truth.

Mac.   I think not of them :
Yet when we can entreat an hour to serve,
We would spend it in some words upon that business,
If you would grant the time.

Ban.   At your kind'st leisure.

Mac. If you shall cleave to my consent, when 'tis,
It shall make honour for you.

Ban.   So I lose none,
In seeking to augment it, but still keep
My bosom franchis'd, and allegiance clear,
I shall be counsell'd.

Mac.   Good repose the while !

Ban. Thanks, sir : the like to you !   30

Exeunt Banquo and Fleance

Mac. Go bid thy mistress, when my drink is ready,
　　　She strike upon the bell. Get thee to bed.

Exit Servant

　　　Is this a dagger, which I see before me,
　　　The handle toward my hand ? Come, let me clutch
　　　　　thee.
　　　I have thee not, and yet I see thee still.
　　　Art thou not, fatal vision, sensible
　　　To feeling, as to sight ? or art thou but
　　　A dagger of the mind, a false creation,
　　　Proceeding from the heat-oppressed brain ?
　　　I see thee yet, in form as palpable   40
　　　As this which now I draw.
　　　Thou marshall'st me the way that I was going,
　　　And such an instrument I was to use.
　　　Mine eyes are made the fools o' the other senses,
　　　Or else worth all the rest : I see thee still ;
　　　And on thy blade, and dudgeon, gouts of blood,
　　　Which was not so before. There 's no such thing :
　　　It is the bloody business, which informs
　　　Thus to mine eyes. Now o'er the one half-world
　　　Nature seems dead, and wicked dreams abuse   50
　　　The curtain'd sleep ; witchcraft celebrates

27

Pale Hecat's offerings ; and wither'd murder,
Alarum'd by his sentinel, the wolf,
Whose howl 's his watch, thus with his stealthy pace,
With Tarquin's ravishing strides, towards his design †
Moves like a ghost. Thou sure and firm-set earth,
Hear not my steps, which way they walk, for fear
Thy very stones prate of my whereabout,
And take the present horror from the time,
Which now suits with it. Whiles I threat, he lives : 60
Words to the heat of deeds too cold breath gives.

A bell rings

I go, and it is done : the bell invites me.
Hear it not, Duncan, for it is a knell
That summons thee to heaven, or to hell.   *Exit*

Enter Lady Macbeth

L.M. That which hath made them drunk hath made me
    bold ;
    What hath quench'd them hath given me fire. Hark !
    Peace !
    It was the owl that shriek'd, the fatal bellman,
    Which gives the stern'st good-night. He is about it,

The doors are open : and the surfeited grooms
Do mock their charge with snores : I have drugg'd
    their possets,
That death and nature do contend about them,
Whether they live or die.

Mac.   (*within*) Who's there ? what ho !

L.M. Alack, I am afraid they have awak'd,
And 'tis not done : the attempt, and not the deed,   10
Confounds us. Hark ! I laid their daggers ready,
He could not miss 'em. Had he not resembled
My father as he slept, I had done 't.

               Enter Macbeth

                   My husband ?

Mac. I have done the deed. Didst thou not hear a noise ?

L.M. I heard the owl scream and the crickets cry.
    Did not you speak ?

Mac.   When ?

L.M.   Now.

Mac.   As I descended ?

L.M. Ay.

Mac. Hark !
    Who lies i' the second chamber ?

L.M.   Donalbain.

Mac. This is a sorry sight.   *Looking on his hands*   20

L.M. A foolish thought, to say a sorry sight.

Mac. There's one did laugh in's sleep, and one cried
      'Murder!'
    That they did wake each other: I stood and heard
      them:
    But they did say their prayers, and address'd them
    Again to sleep.

L.M.   There are two lodg'd together.

Mac. One cried, 'God bless us!', and 'Amen' the
      other,
    As they had seen me with these hangman's hands:
    Listening their fear, I could not say 'Amen,'
    When they did say 'God bless us!'

L.M. Consider it not so deeply.   30

Mac. But wherefore could not I pronounce 'Amen'?
    I had most need of blessing, and 'Amen'
    Stuck in my throat.

L.M.   These deeds must not be thought
    After these ways; so, it will make us mad.

Mac. Methought I heard a voice cry 'Sleep no more!
    Macbeth does murder sleep'—the innocent sleep,
    Sleep that knits up the ravell'd sleeve of care,
    The death of each day's life, sore labour's bath,
    Balm of hurt minds, great nature's second course,
    Chief nourisher in life's feast,—

L.M.   What do you mean? 40

Mac. Still it cried ' Sleep no more ! ' to all the house :
   ' Glamis hath murder'd sleep, and therefore Cawdor
   Shall sleep no more : Macbeth shall sleep no more.'

L.M. Who was it, that thus cried ?   Why, worthy thane,
   You do unbend your noble strength, to think
   So brainsickly of things.   Go get some water,
   And wash this filthy witness from your hand.
   Why did you bring these daggers from the place ?
   They must lie there : go carry them, and smear
   The sleepy grooms with blood.

Mac.   I 'll go no more :   50
   I am afraid, to think what I have done ;
   Look on 't again I dare not.

L.M.   Infirm of purpose !
   Give me the daggers : the sleeping, and the dead,
   Are but as pictures : 'tis the eye of childhood,
   That fears a painted devil.   If he do bleed,
   I 'll gild the faces of the grooms withal,
   For it must seem their guilt.

                    Exit.   Knocking within

Mac.   Whence is that knocking ?
   How is 't with me, when every noise appals me ?
   What hands are here ? ha ! they pluck out mine eyes !
   Will all great Neptune's ocean wash this blood   60
   Clean from my hand ?   No ; this my hand will rather

The multitudinous seas incarnadine,
Making the green one red.   †

Re-enter Lady Macbeth

L.M. My hands are of your colour : but I shame
To wear a heart so white. (*Knocking within.*) I hear
a knocking
At the south entry : retire we to our chamber :
A little water clears us of this deed :
How easy is it then !   Your constancy
Hath left you unattended. (*Knocking within.*) Hark !
more knocking :
Get on your nightgown, lest occasion call us   7c
And show us to be watchers : be not lost
So poorly in your thoughts.

Mac. To know my deed, 'twere best not know myself.

Knocking within

Wake Duncan with thy knocking !   I would thou
could'st !   *Exeunt*

Enter a Porter.   Knocking within

Por. Here's a knocking indeed !   If a man were porter
of hell-gate, he should have old turning the key.
(*Knocking within.*)   Knock, knock, knock !   Who's

32

there, i' the name of Beelzebub? Here's a farmer,
that hang'd himself on th' expectation of plenty:
come in time; have napkins enow about you; here
you 'll sweat for 't. (*Knocking within*.) Knock, knock!
Who's there, in th'other devil's name? Faith,
here's an equivocator, that could swear in both the †
scales against either scale, who committed treason   10
enough for God's sake, yet could not equivocate
to heaven: O, come in, equivocator. (*Knocking
within*.) Knock, knock, knock! Who's there?
Faith, here's an English tailor come hither, for
stealing out of a French hose: come in tailor,
here you may roast your goose. (*Knocking within*.)
Knock, knock; never at quiet! What are you?
But this place is too cold for hell. I 'll devil-
porter it no further: I had thought to have let in
some of all professions, that go the primrose way to   20
the everlasting bonfire. (*Knocking within*.) Anon,
anon! I pray you, remember the porter.

Opens the gate

Enter Macduff and Lennox

Macd. Was it so late, friend, ere you went to bed,
That you do lie so late?

Por. Faith, sir, we were carousing till the second cock:
and drink, sir, is a great provoker of three things.

33

Macd. What three things does drink especially provoke?

Por. Marry, sir, nose-painting, sleep, and urine. Lechery,
sir, it provokes and unprovokes; it provokes the
desire, but it takes away the performance: therefore 30
much drink may be said to be an equivocator with
lechery: it makes him and it mars him; it sets him
on and it takes him off; it persuades him and dis-
heartens him; makes him stand to, and not stand
to; in conclusion, equivocates him in a sleep, and
giving him the lie, leaves him.

Macd. I believe drink gave thee the lie last night.

Por. That it did, sir, i' the very throat on me: but I
requited him for his lie, and, I think, being too
strong for him, though he took up my legs some- 40
time, yet I made a shift to cast him.

Macd. Is thy master stirring?

Enter Macbeth

Our knocking has awak'd him; here he comes.

Len. Good morrow, noble sir.

Mac.   Good morrow, both.

Macd. Is the king stirring, worthy thane?

Mac.   Not yet.

Macd. He did command me to call timely on him;
I have almost slipp'd the hour.

Mac.   I 'll bring you to him.

Macd. I know this is a joyful trouble to you ;
　　But yet 'tis one.

Mac. The labour we delight in physics pain :　　　50
　　This is the door.

Macd.　　　　　　I 'll make so bold to call,
　　For 'tis my limited service.　　　　　*Exit*

Len. Goes the king hence to-day ?

Mac.　　　　　　He does : he did appoint so.

Len. The night has been unruly : where we lay,
　　Our chimneys were blown down, and, as they say,
　　Lamentings heard i' the air, strange screams of death,
　　And prophesying, with accents terrible,
　　Of dire combustion, and confus'd events,
　　New hatch'd to the woful time : the obscure bird
　　Clamour'd the livelong night : some say, the earth　　60
　　Was feverous, and did shake.

Mac.　　　　　　　　'Twas a rough night.

Len. My young remembrance cannot parallel
　　A fellow to it.

　　　　　　　Re-enter Macduff

Macd. O horror, horror, horror !　Tongue nor heart
　　Cannot conceive nor name thee.

Mac. ⎫
Len. ⎭　　　　　What 's the matter ?

Macd. Confusion now hath made his masterpiece.

35

Most sacrilegious murder hath broke ope
The Lord's anointed temple, and stole thence
The life o' the building.

Mac.   What is 't you say ? the life ?

Len. Mean you his majesty ?   70

Macd. Approach the chamber, and destroy your sight
With a new Gorgon : do not bid me speak ;
See, and then speak yourselves.

                 Exeunt Macbeth and Lennox

                   Awake, awake !
Ring the alarum-bell. Murder and treason !
Banquo and Donalbain ! Malcolm, awake !
Shake off this downy sleep, death's counterfeit,
And look on death itself ! up, up, and see
The great doom's image ! Malcolm ! Banquo !
As from your graves rise up, and walk like sprites,
To countenance this horror. Ring the bell.   80

                   Bell rings

         Enter Lady Macbeth

L.M. What's the business,
That such a hideous trumpet calls to parley
The sleepers of the house ? speak, speak !

Macd.   O gentle lady,
'Tis not for you to hear what I can speak :
The repetition, in a woman's ear,

Would murder as it fell.

Enter Banquo

O Banquo, Banquo !

Our royal master 's murder'd.

L.M.   Woe, alas !

What, in our house ?

Ban.   Too cruel, any where.

Dear Duff, I prithee, contradict thyself,

And say it is not so.   90

Re-enter Macbeth and Lennox, with Ross

Mac. Had I but died an hour before this chance,

I had lived a blessed time ; for from this instant

There 's nothing serious in mortality :

All is but toys : renown and grace is dead ;

The wine of life is drawn, and the mere lees

Is left this vault to brag of.

Enter Malcolm and Donalbain

Don. What is amiss ?

Mac.   You are, and do not know 't :

The spring, the head, the fountain of your blood

Is stopp'd, the very source of it is stopp'd.

Macd. Your royal father 's murder'd.

Mal.   O, by whom ?   100

Len. Those of his chamber, as it seem'd, had done 't :

Their hands and faces were all badg'd with blood,

37

So were their daggers, which unwip'd we found
Upon their pillows :
They star'd, and were distracted ; no man's life
Was to be trusted with them.

Mac. O, yet I do repent me of my fury,
That I did kill them.

Macd.   Wherefore did you so ?

Mac. Who can be wise, amaz'd, temperate, and furious,
Loyal, and neutral, in a moment ?   No man :   110
The expedition of my violent love
Outran the pauser, reason.   Here lay Duncan,
His silver skin lac'd with his golden blood,
And his gash'd stabs look'd like a breach in nature
For ruin's wasteful entrance : there the murderers,
Steep'd in the colours of their trade ; their daggers
Unmannerly breech'd with gore : who could refrain,
That had a heart to love, and in that heart
Courage to make 's love known ?

L.M.   Help me hence, ho !

Macd. Look to the lady.

Mal.   (*aside to Don.*) Why do we hold our tongues,   120
That most may claim this argument for ours ?

Don. (*aside to Mal.*) What should be spoken here, where our
       fate,
Hid in an auger-hole, may rush, and seize us ?

Let 's away ;
Our tears are not yet brew'd.

Mal.   (*aside to Don.*) Nor our strong sorrow
Upon the foot of motion.

Ban.   Look to the lady :
               Lady Macbeth is carried out

And when we have our naked frailties hid,
That suffer in exposure, let us meet,
And question this most bloody piece of work,
To know it further.   Fears and scruples shake us :   130
In the great hand of God I stand, and thence
Against the undivulg'd pretence I fight
Of treasonous malice.

Macd.   And so do I.

All.   So all.

Mac. Let 's briefly put on manly readiness,
And meet i' the hall together.

All.   Well contented.
       Exeunt all but Malcolm and Donalbain

Mal. What will you do ?   Let 's not consort with them :
To show an unfelt sorrow is an office
Which the false man does easy.   I 'll to England.

Don. To Ireland, I ;   our separated fortune
Shall keep us both the safer :   where we are,   140
There 's daggers in men's smiles :   the near in blood,

The nearer bloody.

Mal.   This murderous shaft that's shot
Hath not yet lighted, and our safest way
Is to avoid the aim.   Therefore to horse;
And let us not be dainty of leave-taking,
But shift away: there's warrant in that theft
Which steals itself, when there's no mercy left.

Exeunt

Enter Ross with an old Man

Old Man. Threescore and ten I can remember well,
Within the volume of which time I have seen
Hours dreadful and things strange: but this sore
    night
Hath trifled former knowings.

Ross.   Ah, good father,
Thou seest the heavens, as troubled with man's act,
Threatens his bloody stage: by the clock 'tis day,
And yet dark night strangles the travelling lamp:
Is 't night's predominance, or the day's shame,
That darkness does the face of earth entomb
When living light should kiss it?

Old Man.   'Tis unnatural,   10
Even like the deed that's done.   On Tuesday last,
A falcon towering in her pride of place
Was by a mousing owl hawk'd at, and kill'd.

Ross. And Duncan's horses (a thing most strange and
        certain)
Beauteous, and swift, the minions of their race,
Turn'd wild in nature, broke their stalls, flung out,
Contending 'gainst obedience, as they would
Make war with mankind.

Old Man.   'Tis said they ate each other.

Ross. They did so ; to the amazement of mine eyes,
That look'd upon 't.

                    Enter Macduff

                        Here comes the good Macduff.   20
How goes the world, sir, now ?

Macd.   Why, see you not ?

Ross. Is 't known who did this more than bloody deed ?

Macd. Those that Macbeth hath slain.

Ross.   Alas, the day !
What good could they pretend ?

Macd.   They were suborn'd :
Malcolm and Donalbain, the king's two sons,
Are stol'n away and fled, which puts upon them
Suspicion of the deed.

Ross.   'Gainst nature still :
    Thriftless ambition, that wilt ravin up
    Thine own lives' means ! Then 'tis most like
    The sovereignty will fall upon Macbeth.   3

Macd. He is already nam'd, and gone to Scone
    To be invested.

Ross.   Where is Duncan's body ?

Macd. Carried to Colme-kill,
    The sacred storehouse of his predecessors,
    And guardian of their bones.

Ross.   Will you to Scone ?

Macd. No, cousin, I 'll to Fife.

Ross.   Well, I will thither.

Macd. Well, may you see things well done there : adieu
    Lest our old robes sit easier than our new !

Ross. Farewell, father.

Old Man. God's benison go with you, and with those   4
    That would make good of bad and friends of foes !

                                   Exeunt

Act Third

SCENES I AND II

Forres.   The palace

Enter Banquo

Ban. Thou hast it now, king, Cawdor, Glamis, all,
   As the weird women promis'd, and I fear
   Thou play'dst most foully for 't : yet it was said
   It should not stand in thy posterity,
   But that myself should be the root and father
   Of many kings.   If there come truth from them,
   As upon thee, Macbeth, their speeches shine,
   Why, by the verities on thee made good,
   May they not be my oracles as well
   And set me up in hope ?   But hush, no more.   10
   *Sennet sounded.   Enter Macbeth, as king, Lady Macbeth,
     as queen, Lennox, Ross, Lords, Ladies, and Attendants*
Mac. Here 's our chief guest.
L.M.   If he had been forgotten,
   It had been as a gap in our great feast,
   And all-thing unbecoming.
Mac. To-night we hold a solemn supper, sir,

43

And I'll request your presence.

Ban.   Let your highness
Command upon me, to the which my duties
Are with a most indissoluble tie
For ever knit.

Mac. Ride you this afternoon?

Ban. Ay, my good lord.   20

Mac. We should have else desir'd your good advice,
(Which still hath been both grave and prosperous)
In this day's council; but we'll take to-morrow.
Is 't far you ride?

Ban. As far, my lord, as will fill up the time
'Twixt this and supper: go not my horse the better,
I must become a borrower of the night,
For a dark hour or twain.

Mac.   Fail not our feast.

Ban. My lord, I will not.

Mac. We hear our bloody cousins are bestow'd   30
In England, and in Ireland, not confessing
Their cruel parricide, filling their hearers
With strange invention.   But of that to-morrow,
When therewithal we shall have cause of state
Craving us jointly.   Hie you to horse: adieu,
Till you return at night.   Goes Fleance with you?

Ban. Ay, my good lord: our time does call upon 's.

44

Mac. I wish your horses swift, and sure of foot,
    And so I do commend you to their backs.
    Farewell.   *Exit Banquo* 40
    Let every man be master of his time
    Till seven at night, to make society
    The sweeter welcome ; we will keep ourself
    Till supper-time alone : while then, God be with you !
                Exeunt all but Macbeth and an Attendant
    Sirrah, a word with you : attend those men
    Our pleasure ?
Att. They are, my lord, without the palace-gate.
Mac. Bring them before us.   *Exit Attendant*
                    To be thus is nothing ;
    But to be safely thus : our fears in Banquo
    Stick deep, and in his royalty of nature   50
    Reigns that which would be fear'd : 'tis much he
        dares,
    And, to that dauntless temper of his mind,
    He hath a wisdom, that doth guide his valour
    To act in safety.   There is none but he
    Whose being I do fear : and under him
    My Genius is rebuk'd, as it is said
    Mark Antony's was by Cæsar.   He chid the sisters,
    When first they put the name of king upon me,
    And bade them speak to him.   Then prophet-like

They hail'd him father to a line of kings.   60
Upon my head they plac'd a fruitless crown,
And put a barren sceptre in my gripe,
Thence to be wrench'd with an unlineal hand,
No son of mine succeeding.   If 't be so,
For Banquo's issue have I fil'd my mind,
For them the gracious Duncan have I murder'd,
Put rancours in the vessel of my peace
Only for them, and mine eternal jewel
Given to the common enemy of man,
To make them kings, the seed of Banquo kings !   70
Rather than so, come fate into the list,
And champion me to the utterance !   Who 's there ?

Re-enter Attendant, with two Murderers

Now go to the door, and stay there till we call.

Exit Attendant

Was it not yesterday we spoke together ?
1.*M.*It was, so please your highness.
Mac.   Well then, now
Have you consider'd of my speeches ?   Know
That it was he in the times past which held you
So under fortune, which you thought had been
Our innocent self : this I made good to you,
In our last conference, pass'd in probation with you ;   80

How you were borne in hand, how cross'd; the
    instruments;
Who wrought with them; and all things else that
    might
To half a soul, and to a notion craz'd,
Say 'Thus did Banquo.'

.M.   You made it known to us.

Mac. I did so; and went further, which is now
    Our point of second meeting. Do you find
    Your patience so predominant in your nature,
    That you can let this go? Are you so gospell'd,
    To pray for this good man, and for his issue,
    Whose heavy hand hath bow'd you to the grave,   90
    And beggar'd yours for ever?

.M.   We are men, my liege.

Mac. Ay, in the catalogue ye go for men,
    As hounds, and greyhounds, mongrels, spaniels, curs,
    Shoughs, water-rugs, and demi-wolves, are clept
    All by the name of dogs: the valued file
    Distinguishes the swift, the slow, the subtle,
    The housekeeper, the hunter, every one
    According to the gift which bounteous nature
    Hath in him clos'd, whereby he does receive
    Particular addition, from the bill   100
    That writes them all alike: and so of men.

Now if you have a station in the file,
Not i' the worst rank of manhood, say it,
And I will put that business in your bosoms,
Whose execution takes your enemy off,
Grapples you to the heart and love of us,
Who wear our health but sickly in his life,
Which in his death were perfect.

2.*M.*   I am one, my liege,
Whom the vile blows and buffets of the world
Hath so incens'd, that I am reckless what   110
I do to spite the world.

1.*M.*   And I another,
So weary with disasters, tugg'd with fortune,
That I would set my life on any chance,
To mend it, or be rid on 't.

Mac.   Both of you
Know Banquo was your enemy.

Both M.   True, my lord.

Mac. So is he mine ; and in such bloody distance,
That every minute of his being thrusts
Against my near'st of life : and though I could
With barefac'd power sweep him from my sight,
And bid my will avouch it, yet I must not,   120
For certain friends that are both his, and mine,
Whose loves I may not drop, but wail his fall

Who I myself struck down : and thence it is
That I to your assistance do make love,
Masking the business from the common eye,
For sundry weighty reasons.

2.*M.*   We shall, my lord,
Perform what you command us.

1.*M.*   Though our lives—

Mac. Your spirits shine through you.   Within this hour,
            at most,
I will advise you where to plant yourselves,
Acquaint you with the perfect spy o' the time,   †
The moment on 't, for 't must be done to-night,   131
And something from the palace ; always thought,
That I require a clearness ; and with him,
To leave no rubs nor botches in the work,
Fleance, his son, that keeps him company,
Whose absence is no less material to me
Than is his father's, must embrace the fate
Of that dark hour : resolve yourselves apart,
I 'll come to you anon.

Both M.   We are resolv'd, my lord.

Mac. I 'll call upon you straight : abide within,   140

                    Exeunt Murderers

It is concluded : Banquo, thy soul's flight,
If it find heaven, must find it out to-night.   *Exit*

Enter Lady Macbeth and a Servant

L.M. Is Banquo gone from court?

Ser. Ay, madam, but returns again to-night.

L.M. Say to the king, I would attend his leisure
For a few words.

Ser.   Madam, I will.   *Exit*

L.M.   Nought 's had, all 's spent,
Where our desire is got without content:
'Tis safer to be that which we destroy
Than by destruction dwell in doubtful joy.

Enter Macbeth

How now, my lord, why do you keep alone,
Of sorriest fancies your companions making,
Using those thoughts which should indeed have died   10
With them they think on?   Things without all remedy
Should be without regard: what 's done, is done.

Mac. We have scotch'd the snake, not kill'd it: †
She 'll close, and be herself, whilst our poor malice
Remains in danger of her former tooth.
But let the frame of things disjoint, both the worlds
     suffer,
Ere we will eat our meal in fear, and sleep
In the affliction of these terrible dreams,

That shake us nightly : better be with the dead,
Whom we, to gain our peace, have sent to peace,   20
Than on the torture of the mind to lie
In restless ecstasy.   Duncan is in his grave :
After life's fitful fever, he sleeps well,
Treason has done his worst : nor steel, nor poison,
Malice domestic, foreign levy, nothing,
Can touch him further.

L.M.   Come on ;
Gentle my lord, sleek o'er your rugged looks,
Be bright and jovial among your guests to-night.

Mac. So shall I, love, and so, I pray, be you :
Let your remembrance apply to Banquo,   30
Present him eminence, both with eye and tongue :
Unsafe the while, that we   †
Must lave our honours in these flattering streams,
And make our faces vizards to our hearts,
Disguising what they are.

L.M.   You must leave this.

Mac. O, full of scorpions is my mind, dear wife !
Thou know'st that Banquo, and his Fleance, lives.

L.M. But in them nature's copy 's not eterne.

Mac. There 's comfort yet, they are assailable,
Then be thou jocund : ere the bat hath flown   40
His cloister'd flight, ere to black Hecat's summons

The shard-borne beetle, with his drowsy hums,
Hath rung night's yawning peal, there shall be done
A deed of dreadful note.

L.M.   What's to be done?

Mac. Be innocent of the knowledge, dearest chuck,
Till thou applaud the deed. Come, seeling night,
Scarf up the tender eye of pitiful day,
And with thy bloody and invisible hand
Cancel and tear to pieces that great bond
Which keeps me pale! Light thickens, and the
     crow   50
Makes wing to the rooky wood:
Good things of day begin to droop and drowse,
Whiles night's black agents to their preys do rouse.
Thou marvell'st at my words: but hold thee still;
Things bad begun make strong themselves by ill:
So, prithee go with me.   *Exeunt*

SCENE III

A park near the palace

Enter three Murderers   †

1.M. But who did bid thee join with us?
3.M.   Macbeth.

2.M. He needs not our mistrust, since he delivers
　　　Our offices, and what we have to do,
　　　To the direction just.

1.M. 　　　　　　　Then stand with us :
　　　The west yet glimmers with some streaks of day :
　　　Now spurs the lated traveller apace,
　　　To gain the timely inn, and near approaches
　　　The subject of our watch.

3.M. 　　　　　　　Hark ! I hear horses.

Ban. (within) Give us a light there, ho !

2.M. 　　　　　　　Then 'tis he : the rest,
　　　That are within the note of expectation,　　　　10
　　　Already are i' the court.

1.M. 　　　　　　His horses go about.

3.M. Almost a mile : but he does usually—
　　　So all men do—from hence to the palace gate
　　　Make it their walk.

2.M. 　　　　A light, a light !

　　　　　Enter Banquo, and Fleance with a torch

3.M. 　　　　　　　'Tis he.

1.M. Stand to 't.

Ban. It will be rain to-night.

1.M. 　　　　　Let it come down.

　　　　　　　　　　They set upon Banquo

Ban. O, treachery ! Fly, good Fleance, fly, fly, fly !

Thou mayst revenge.   O slave !

Dies.   Fleance escapes

3.*M.* Who did strike out the light ?

1.*M.*   Was 't not the way ?

3.*M.* There 's but one down ; the son is fled.

2.*M.*   We have lost   20

Best half of our affair.

1.*M.* Well, let 's away, and say how much is done.

Exeunt

SCENE IV

Hall in the palace

*A banquet prepared.   Enter Macbeth, Lady Macbeth,
Ross, Lennox, Lords, and Attendants*

Mac. You know your own degrees, sit down : at first
And last the hearty welcome.

Lords.   Thanks to your majesty.

Mac. Ourself will mingle with society,
And play the humble host.
Our hostess keeps her state, but in best time
We will require her welcome.

L.M. Pronounce it for me, sir, to all our friends,
For my heart speaks, they are welcome.

Enter First Murderer to the door

Mac. See, they encounter thee with their hearts' thanks.
　　Both sides are even : here I 'll sit i' the midst,　　　　10
　　Be large in mirth, anon we 'll drink a measure
　　The table round. (*Approaching the door*) There 's
　　　　blood upon thy face.

Mur. 'Tis Banquo's then.

Mac. 'Tis better thee without than he within.
　　Is he dispatch'd ?

Mur. My lord, his throat is cut, that I did for him.

Mac. Thou art the best o' the cut-throats, yet he 's good
　　That did the like for Fleance : if thou didst it,
　　Thou art the nonpareil.

Mur. 　　　　　　　Most royal sir,
　　Fleance is 'scap'd.　　　　　　　　　　　　　　　20

Mac. (*aside*) Then comes my fit again : I had else been
　　　　perfect,
　　Whole as the marble, founded as the rock,
　　As broad, and general, as the casing air :
　　But now I am cabin'd, cribb'd, confin'd, bound in
　　To saucy doubts and fears.—But Banquo 's safe ?

Mur. Ay, my good lord : safe in a ditch he bides,
　　With twenty trenched gashes on his head ;
　　The least a death to nature.

Mac. 　　　　　　　Thanks for that.

55

> (*aside*) There the grown serpent lies, the worm that 's
>   fled
> Hath nature that in time will venom breed,   30
> No teeth for the present. Get thee gone, to-morrow
> We 'll hear ourselves again.   *Exit Murderer*

L.M.   My royal lord,
> You do not give the cheer, the feast is sold   †
> That is not often vouch'd, while 'tis a making :
> 'Tis given, with welcome : to feed were best at
>   home ;
> From thence, the sauce to meat is ceremony,
> Meeting were bare without it.
> *The Ghost of Banquo enters, and sits in Macbeth's place*

Mac.   Sweet remembrancer !
> Now good digestion wait on appetite,
> And health on both !

Len.   May 't please your highness sit.

Mac. Here had we now our country's honour roof'd,   40
> Were the grac'd person of our Banquo present ;
> Who may I rather challenge for unkindness,
> Than pity for mischance !

Ross.   His absence, sir,
> Lays blame upon his promise.   Please 't your high-
>   ness
> To grace us with your royal company ?

Mac. The table's full.

Len.   Here is a place reserv'd, sir.

Mac. Where?

Len. Here, my good lord. What is't that moves your
      highness?

Mac. Which of you have done this?

Lords.   What, my good lord?

Mac. Thou canst not say I did it: never shake   50
      Thy gory locks at me.

Ross. Gentlemen, rise, his highness is not well.

L.M. Sit, worthy friends: my lord is often thus,
      And hath been from his youth: pray you, keep seat,
      The fit is momentary, upon a thought
      He will again be well. If much you note him,
      You shall offend him, and extend his passion,
      Feed, and regard him not. Are you a man?

Mac. Ay, and a bold one, that dare look on that
      Which might appal the devil.

L.M.   O proper stuff!   60
      This is the very painting of your fear:
      This is the air-drawn dagger which you said
      Led you to Duncan. O, these flaws and starts,
      (Impostors to true fear) would well become
      A woman's story at a winter's fire,
      Authoriz'd by her grandam. Shame itself,

²¹ *f*   57

Why do you make such faces ? When all 's done,
You look but on a stool.

*Mac.*Prithee see there ! behold ! look ! lo ! how say you ?
Why, what care I ? If thou canst nod, speak too.   70
If charnel-houses and our graves must send
Those that we bury back, our monuments
Shall be the maws of kites.   *Exit Ghost*

L.M.   What, quite unmann'd in folly ?

*Mac.*If I stand here, I saw him.

L.M.   Fie, for shame !

*Mac.*Blood hath been shed ere now, i' the olden time,
Ere humane statute purg'd the gentle weal ;
Ay, and since too, murders have been perform'd
Too terrible for the ear : the time has been,
That, when the brains were out, the man would die,
And there an end ; but now they rise again,   80
With twenty mortal murders on their crowns,
And push us from our stools : this is more strange
Than such a murder is.

L.M.   My worthy lord,
Your noble friends do lack you.

Mac.   I do forget.
Do not muse at me, my most worthy friends,
I have a strange infirmity, which is nothing
To those that know me. Come, love and health to all,

Then I 'll sit down.   Give me some wine, fill full.
Re-enter Ghost
I drink to the general joy o' the whole table,
And to our dear friend Banquo, whom we miss ;　　90
Would he were here ! to all and him we thirst,
And all to all.

Lords.　　　　Our duties, and the pledge.

Mac. Avaunt, and quit my sight, let the earth hide thee !
Thy bones are marrowless, thy blood is cold ;
Thou hast no speculation in those eyes
Which thou dost glare with.

L.M.　　　　　Think of this, good peers,
But as a thing of custom : 'tis no other,
Only it spoils the pleasure of the time.

Mac. What man dare, I dare :
Approach thou like the rugged Russian bear,　　100
The arm'd rhinoceros, or the Hyrcan tiger,
Take any shape but that, and my firm nerves
Shall never tremble.   Or be alive again,
And dare me to the desert with thy sword ;
If trembling I inhabit then, protest me
The baby of a girl.   Hence, horrible shadow !
Unreal mockery, hence !　　　*Exit Ghost*
　　　　　　Why so, being gone,
I am a man again : pray you, sit still.

*L.M.*You have displac'd the mirth, broke the good
    meeting,
    With most admir'd disorder.

Mac.   Can such things be,   110
    And overcome us like a summer's cloud,
    Without our special wonder ? You make me
      strange
    Even to the disposition that I owe,
    When now I think you can behold such sights,
    And keep the natural ruby of your cheeks,
    When mine is blanch'd with fear.

Ross.   What sights, my lord ?

*L.M.*I pray you, speak not ; he grows worse and worse ;
    Question enrages him : at once, good night.
    Stand not upon the order of your going,
    But go at once.

Len.   Good night, and better health   120
    Attend his majesty !

L.M.   A kind good night to all !
       Exeunt all but Macbeth and Lady Macbeth

*Mac.*It will have blood they say : blood will have blood :
    Stones have been known to move, and trees to speak ;
    Augures and understood relations have
    By maggot-pies, and choughs, and rooks brought
      forth

The secret'st man of blood.   What is the night?

*L.M.*Almost at odds with morning, which is which.

*Mac.*How say'st thou, that Macduff denies his person   †
    At our great bidding?

L.M.   Did you send to him, sir?

*Mac.*I hear it by the way: but I will send: 130
    There 's not a one of them but in his house
    I keep a servant fee'd.   I will to-morrow
    (And betimes I will) to the weird sisters:
    More shall they speak; for now I am bent to know,
    By the worst means, the worst, for mine own good,
    All causes shall give way: I am in blood
    Stepp'd in so far, that should I wade no more,
    Returning were as tedious as go o'er:
    Strange things I have in head, that will to hand,
    Which must be acted, ere they may be scann'd.   140

*L.M.*You lack the season of all natures, sleep.

*Mac.*Come, we 'll to sleep.   My strange and self-abuse
    Is the initiate fear, that wants hard use:
    We are yet but young in deed.   *Exeunt*

SCENE V

The heath

Thunder.   Enter the three Witches, meeting Hecate

1. *W.* Why, how now, Hecat? you look angerly.

Hec. Have I not reason, beldams as you are?
      Saucy, and over-bold, how did you dare
      To trade and traffic with Macbeth
      In riddles, and affairs of death;
      And I, the mistress of your charms,
      The close contriver of all harms,
      Was never call'd to bear my part,
      Or show the glory of our art?
      And, which is worse, all you have done   10
      Hath been but for a wayward son,
      Spiteful, and wrathful, who (as others do)
      Loves for his own ends, not for you.
      But make amends now: get you gone,
      And at the pit of Acheron
      Meet me i' the morning: thither he
      Will come, to know his destiny:
      Your vessels, and your spells provide,
      Your charms, and every thing beside;
      I am for the air; this night I 'll spend   20

Unto a dismal and a fatal end.
Great business must be wrought ere noon :
Upon the corner of the moon
There hangs a vaporous drop, profound,
I 'll catch it ere it come to ground ;
And that, distill'd by magic sleights,
Shall raise such artificial sprites,
As by the strength of their illusion
Shall draw him on to his confusion.
He shall spurn fate, scorn death, and bear   30
His hopes 'bove wisdom, grace, and fear :
And you all know, security
Is mortals' chiefest enemy.   *Music*
Hark ! I am call'd ; my little spirit, see,
Sits in a foggy cloud, and stays for me.   *Exit*
          A song within : ' Come away, come away,' &c.
*I.W.*Come, let 's make haste ; she 'll soon be back again.
                                        Exeunt

SCENE VI

Forres.   The palace

Enter Lennox and another Lord

Len. My former speeches have but hit your thoughts,
    Which can interpret farther : only I say

Things have been strangely borne.   The gracious
    Duncan
Was pitied of Macbeth : marry, he was dead :
And the right-valiant Banquo walk'd too late,
Whom (you may say if 't please you) Fleance kill'd,
For Fleance fled : men must not walk too late.
Who cannot want the thought, how monstrous
It was for Malcolm and for Donalbain
To kill their gracious father ? damned fact,   10
How it did grieve Macbeth ! did he not straight,
In pious rage, the two delinquents tear,
That were the slaves of drink, and thralls of sleep ?
Was not that nobly done ?   Ay, and wisely too ;
For 'twould have anger'd any heart alive
To hear the men deny 't.   So that I say,
He has borne all things well, and I do think
That, had he Duncan's sons under his key,
(As, an 't please heaven, he shall not) they should
    find
What 'twere to kill a father ; so should Fleance.   20
But, peace ! for from broad words, and 'cause he
    fail'd
His presence at the tyrant's feast, I hear
Macduff lives in disgrace : sir, can you tell
Where he bestows himself ?

Lord.   The son of Duncan
   (From whom this tyrant holds the due of birth)
   Lives in the English court, and is receiv'd
   Of the most pious Edward with such grace
   That the malevolence of fortune nothing
   Takes from his high respect. Thither Macduff is gone,
   To pray the holy king, upon his aid   30
   To wake Northumberland and warlike Siward,
   That by the help of these (with Him above
   To ratify the work) we may again
   Give to our tables meat, sleep to our nights,
   Free from our feasts and banquets bloody knives,
   Do faithful homage, and receive free honours,
   All which we pine for now.   And this report
   Hath so exasperate the king that he
   Prepares for some attempt of war.

Len.   Sent he to Macduff?

Lord. He did : and with an absolute ' Sir, not I,'   40
   The cloudy messenger turns me his back,
   And hums ; as who should say ' You 'll rue the time
   That clogs me with this answer.'

Len.   And that well might
   Advise him to a caution, to hold what distance
   His wisdom can provide.   Some holy angel
   Fly to the court of England, and unfold

His message ere he come, that a swift blessing
May soon return to this our suffering country
Under a hand accurs'd !

Lord.   I 'll send my prayers with him.

Exeunt

Act Fourth

SCENE I

A cavern.   In the middle, a boiling cauldron

Thunder.   Enter the three Witches

1.*W*.Thrice the brinded cat hath mew'd.

2.*W*.Thrice, and once the hedge-pig whin'd.

3.*W*.Harpier cries ' 'Tis time, 'tis time.'

1.*W*.Round about the cauldron go :
    In the poison'd entrails throw ;
    Toad, that under cold stone
    Days and nights has thirty one
    Swelter'd venom sleeping got,
    Boil thou first i' the charmed pot.

All. Double, double, toil and trouble ;
    Fire burn, and cauldron bubble.

2.*W*.Fillet of a fenny snake,

10

In the cauldron boil and bake ;
Eye of newt, and toe of frog,
Wool of bat, and tongue of dog ;
Adder's fork, and blind-worm's sting,
Lizard's leg, and howlet's wing ;
For a charm of powerful trouble,
Like a hell-broth, boil and bubble.
All. Double, double, toil and trouble,   20
Fire burn, and cauldron bubble.
3.*W*.Scale of dragon, tooth of wolf,
Witches' mummy, maw, and gulf
Of the ravin'd salt-sea shark ;
Root of hemlock, digg'd i' the dark ;
Liver of blaspheming Jew,
Gall of goat, and slips of yew,
Sliver'd in the moon's eclipse ;
Nose of Turk, and Tartar's lips ;
Finger of birth-strangled babe,   30
Ditch-deliver'd by a drab,
Make the gruel thick and slab :
Add thereto a tiger's chaudron,
For the ingredients of our cauldron.
All.Double, double, toil and trouble,
Fire burn, and cauldron bubble.
2.*W*.Cool it with a baboon's blood,

Then the charm is firm and good.
> *Enter Hecate to the other three Witches*

Hec. O, well done ! I commend your pains,
And every one shall share i' the gains :   40
And now about the cauldron sing,
Like elves and fairies in a ring,
Enchanting all that you put in.
> *Music and a song : ' Black spirits,' &c.*

2. W. By the pricking of my thumbs,
Something wicked this way comes :
Open locks,
Whoever knocks !
> *Enter Macbeth*

Mac. How now, you secret, black, and midnight hags ?
What is 't you do ?

All.   A deed without a name.

Mac. I conjure you, by that which you profess,   50
(Howe'er you come to know it) answer me :
Though you untie the winds, and let them fight
Against the churches ; though the yesty waves
Confound and swallow navigation up ;
Though bladed corn be lodg'd, and trees blown down,
Though castles topple on their warders' heads ;
Though palaces and pyramids do slope
Their heads to their foundations ; though the treasure

Of nature's germins tumble all together,
Even till destruction sicken ; answer me   60
To what I ask you.

.*W*.   Speak.

.*W*.   Demand.

.*W*.   We 'll answer.

.*W*.Say, if thou 'dst rather hear it from our mouths,
Or from our masters.

Mac.   Call 'em : let me see 'em.

.*W*.Pour in sow's blood, that hath eaten
Her nine farrow ; grease that 's sweaten
From the murderer's gibbet throw
Into the flame.

All.   Come high or low :
Thyself and office deftly show !

  Thunder. First Apparition : an armed Head

Mac. Tell me, thou unknown power,—

.*W*.   He knows thy thought :
Hear his speech, but say thou nought.   70

.*A*.Macbeth ! Macbeth ! Macbeth ! beware Macduff,
Beware the thane of Fife. Dismiss me : enough.

         Descends

Mac.Whate'er thou art, for thy good caution, thanks ;
Thou hast harp'd my fear aright : but one word more,—

.*W*.He will not be commanded : here 's another,

More potent than the first.

Thunder.   Second Apparition : a bloody Child

2.*A.*Macbeth ! Macbeth ! Macbeth !

*Mac.*Had I three ears, I 'ld hear thee.

2.*A.*Be bloody, bold, and resolute ; laugh to scorn
The power of man : for none of woman born   8o
Shall harm Macbeth.   *Descends*

*Mac.*Then live Macduff : what need I fear of thee ?
But yet I 'll make assurance double sure,
And take a bond of fate : thou shalt not live,
That I may tell pale-hearted fear, it lies ;
And sleep in spite of thunder.

*Thunder.   Third Apparition : a Child crowned, with a tree
in his hand*

What is this,
That rises like the issue of a king,
And wears upon his baby-brow the round
And top of sovereignty ?

All.   Listen, but speak not to 't.

3.*A.*Be lion-mettled, proud, and take no care   9o
Who chafes, who frets, or where conspirers are :
Macbeth shall never vanquish'd be, until
Great Birnam wood to high Dunsinane hill
Shall come against him.   *Descends*

Mac.   That will never be :

Who can impress the forest, bid the tree
Unfix his earth-bound root ? Sweet bodements ! good !
Rebellious dead, rise never, till the wood   †
Of Birnam rise, and our high-plac'd Macbeth
Shall live the lease of nature, pay his breath
To time, and mortal custom.   Yet my heart   100
Throbs to know one thing : tell me, if your art
Can tell so much : shall Banquo's issue ever
Reign in this kingdom ?

All.   Seek to know no more.

Mac. I will be satisfied : deny me this,
And an eternal curse fall on you !   Let me know :
Why sinks that cauldron ? and what noise is this ?

Hautboys

1 W. Show !

2 W. Show !

3 W. Show !

All. Show his eyes, and grieve his heart,   110
Come like shadows, so depart !

*A show of eight Kings, the last with a glass in his hand ;
Banquo's Ghost following*

Mac. Thou art too like the spirit of Banquo : down !
Thy crown does sear mine eye-balls.   And thy hair,
Thou other gold-bound brow, is like the first.
A third, is like the former.   Filthy hags !

Why do you show me this ? A fourth ? Start, eyes !
What, will the line stretch out to the crack of doom ?
Another yet ? A seventh ? I 'll see no more :
And yet the eighth appears, who bears a glass
Which shows me many more ; and some I see   120
That two-fold balls and treble sceptres carry :
Horrible sight ! Now I see 'tis true,
For the blood-bolter'd Banquo smiles upon me,
And points at them for his. What, is this so ?

1. W. Ay, sir, all this is so : but why
Stands Macbeth thus amazedly ?
Come, sisters, cheer we up his sprites,
And show the best of our delights :
I 'll charm the air to give a sound,
While you perform your antic round :   130
That this great king may kindly say,
Our duties did his welcome pay.

Music. The Witches dance, and then
vanish, with Hecate

Mac. Where are they ? Gone ? Let this pernicious hour
Stand aye accursed in the calendar !
Come in, without there !

Enter Lennox

Len.   What 's your grace's will ?
Mac. Saw you the weird sisters ?

72

Len.   No, my lord.

Mac. Came they not by you ?

Len.   No indeed, my lord.

Mac. Infected be the air whereon they ride,
         And damn'd all those that trust them ! I did hear
         The galloping of horse : who was 't came by ?   140

Len. 'Tis two or three, my lord, that bring you word
         Macduff is fled to England.

Mac.   Fled to England ?

Len. Ay, my good lord.

Mac. (*aside*) Time, thou anticipat'st my dread exploits :
         The flighty purpose never is o'ertook
         Unless the deed go with it : from this moment
         The very firstlings of my heart shall be
         The firstlings of my hand. And even now,
         To crown my thoughts with acts, be it thought and
             done :
         The castle of Macduff I will surprise,   150
         Seize upon Fife ; give to the edge o' the sword
         His wife, his babes, and all unfortunate souls
         That trace him in his line. No boasting like a fool,
         This deed I 'll do, before this purpose cool,
         But no more sights !—Where are these gentlemen ?
         Come, bring me where they are.   *Exeunt*

SCENE II

Fife.   Macduff's castle

Enter Lady Macduff, her Son, and Ross

*L.M.*What had he done, to make him fly the land ?

*Ross.*You must have patience, madam.

L.M.   He had none :
    His flight was madness : when our actions do not,
    Our fears do make us traitors.

Ross.   You know not
    Whether it was his wisdom, or his fear.

*L.M.*Wisdom ? to leave his wife, to leave his babes,
    His mansion, and his titles, in a place
    From whence himself does fly ?   He loves us not,
    He wants the natural touch.   For the poor wren
    (The most diminutive of birds) will fight,   10
    Her young ones in her nest, against the owl.
    All is the fear, and nothing is the love ;
    As little is the wisdom, where the flight
    So runs against all reason.

Ross.   My dearest coz,
    I pray you school yourself : but, for your husband,
    He is noble, wise, judicious, and best knows
    The fits o' the season.   I dare not speak much further,

But cruel are the times, when we are traitors
And do not know ourselves ; when we hold rumour
From what we fear, yet know not what we fear,   20
But float upon a wild and violent sea
Each way, and move.   I take my leave of you :   †
Shall not be long but l 'll be here again :
Things at the worst will cease, or else climb upward,
To what they were before.   My pretty cousin,
Blessing upon you !

*L.M.*Father'd he is, and yet he 's fatherless.

*Ross.*I am so much a fool, should I stay longer,
It would be my disgrace and your discomfort :
I take my leave at once.   *Exit*

L.M.   Sirrah, your father 's dead,   30
And what will you do now ?   How will you live ?

Son. As birds do, mother.

L.M.   What, with worms and flies ?

Son. With what I get, I mean, and so do they.

*L.M.*Poor bird, thou 'ldst never fear the net nor lime,
The pitfall, nor the gin.

Son. Why should I, mother ?   Poor birds they are not
          set for.
My father is not dead, for all your saying.

*L.M.*Yes, he is dead : how wilt thou do for a father ?

Son. Nay, how will you do for a husband ?

75

*L.M.*Why, I can buy me twenty at any market.   40

Son. Then you 'll buy 'em to sell again.

*L.M.*Thou speak'st with all thy wit, and yet, i' faith,
    With wit enough for thee.

Son. Was my father a traitor, mother ?

*L.M.*Ay, that he was.

Son. What is a traitor ?

*L.M.*Why, one that swears, and lies.

Son. And be all traitors that do so ?

*L.M.*Every one that does so is a traitor, and must be hang'd.

Son. And must they all be hang'd that swear and lie ?   50

*L.M.*Every one.

Son. Who must hang them ?

*L.M.*Why, the honest men.

Son. Then the liars and swearers are fools ; for there are
    liars and swearers enow to beat the honest men, and
    hang up them.

*L.M.*Now, God help thee, poor monkey !
    But how wilt thou do for a father ?

Son. If he were dead, you 'ld weep for him : if you would
    not, it were a good sign that I should quickly have   60
    a new father.

*L.M.*Poor prattler, how thou talk'st !

Enter a Messenger

*Mes.*Bless you fair dame !   I am not to you known,

Though in your state of honour I am perfect ;
I doubt some danger does approach you nearly :
If you will take a homely man's advice,
Be not found here ; hence, with your little ones.
To fright you thus, methinks I am too savage ;
To do worse to you were fell cruelty,
Which is too nigh your person.   Heaven preserve
    you !   70
I dare abide no longer.   *Exit*

L.M.   Whither should I fly ?
I have done no harm.   But I remember now
I am in this earthly world, where to do harm
Is often laudable, to do good sometime
Accounted dangerous folly : why then, alas,
Do I put up that womanly defence,
To say I have done no harm ?—What are these faces ?

Enter Murderers

1.M. Where is your husband ?

L.M. I hope in no place so unsanctified
    Where such as thou mayst find him.

1.M.   He's a traitor.   80

Son. Thou liest, thou shag-ear'd villain !

1.M.   What, you egg !
                           Stabbing him

Young fry of treachery !

Son.   He has kill'd me, mother :
    Run away, I pray you !   *Dies*
                Exit Lady Macduff, crying ' Murder ! ' †
                        Exeunt murderers, following her

SCENE III

England.   Before the King's palace

Enter Malcolm and Macduff

Mal. Let us seek out some desolate shade, and there
    Weep our sad bosoms empty.

Macd.   Let us rather
    Hold fast the mortal sword, and like good men
    Bestride our down-fall'n birthdom : each new morn
    New widows howl, new orphans cry, new sorrows
    Strike heaven on the face, that it resounds
    As if it felt with Scotland, and yell'd out
    Like syllable of dolour.

Mal.   What I believe, I 'll wail ;
    What know, believe ; and what I can redress,
    As I shall find the time to friend, I will.
    What you have spoke, it may be so perchance.   10
    This tyrant, whose sole name blisters our tongues,
    Was once thought honest : you have lov'd him well ;

He hath not touch'd you yet. I am young; but
    something
You may discern of him through me, and wisdom   †
To offer up a weak, poor, innocent lamb
To appease an angry god.

Macd. I am not treacherous.

Mal.   But Macbeth is.
A good and virtuous nature may recoil
In an imperial charge. But I shall crave your pardon :
That which you are, my thoughts cannot transpose ;   21
Angels are bright still, though the brightest fell :
Though all things foul would wear the brows of grace,
Yet grace must still look so.

Macd.   I have lost my hopes.

Mal. Perchance even there where I did find my doubts.
Why in that rawness left you wife and child,
Those precious motives, those strong knots of love,
Without leave-taking ? I pray you,
Let not my jealousies be your dishonours,
But mine own safeties. You may be rightly just,   30
Whatever I shall think.

Macd.   Bleed, bleed, poor country :
Great tyranny, lay thou thy basis sure,
For goodness dare not check thee : wear thou thy
    wrongs ;

The title is affeer'd.   Fare thee well, lord :
I would not be the villain that thou think'st
For the whole space that's in the tyrant's grasp,
And the rich East to boot.

Mal.   Be not offended :
I speak not as in absolute fear of you :
I think our country sinks beneath the yoke,
It weeps, it bleeds, and each new day a gash   40
Is added to her wounds : I think withal
There would be hands uplifted in my right ;
And here from gracious England have I offer
Of goodly thousands : but for all this,
When I shall tread upon the tyrant's head,
Or wear it on my sword, yet my poor country
Shall have more vices than it had before,
More suffer, and more sundry ways than ever,
By him that shall succeed.

Macd.   What should he be ?

Mal. It is myself I mean : in whom I know   50
All the particulars of vice so grafted
That, when they shall be open'd, black Macbeth
Will seem as pure as snow, and the poor state
Esteem him as a lamb, being compar'd
With my confineless harms.

Macd.   Not in the legions

Of horrid hell can come a devil more damn'd
In evils, to top Macbeth.

Mal.   I grant him bloody,
Luxurious, avaricious, false, deceitful,
Sudden, malicious, smacking of every sin
That has a name : but there's no bottom, none,   60
In my voluptuousness : your wives, your daughters,
Your matrons, and your maids, could not fill up
The cistern of my lust, and my desire
All continent impediments would o'erbear,
That did oppose my will : better Macbeth
Than such an one to reign.

Macd.   Boundless intemperance
In nature is a tyranny ; it hath been
The untimely emptying of the happy throne,
And fall of many kings.   But fear not yet
To take upon you what is yours : you may   70
Convey your pleasures in a spacious plenty,
And yet seem cold, the time you may so hoodwink :
We have willing dames enough ; there cannot be
That vulture in you, to devour so many
As will to greatness dedicate themselves,
Finding it so inclined.

Mal.   With this there grows,
In my most ill-compos'd affection, such

A stanchless avarice, that, were I king,
I should cut off the nobles for their lands,
Desire his jewels, and this other's house :   8(
And my more-having would be as a sauce
To make me hunger more, that I should forge
Quarrels unjust against the good and loyal,
Destroying them for wealth.

Macd.   This avarice
Sticks deeper, grows with more pernicious root
Than summer-seeming lust, and it hath been
The sword of our slain kings : yet do not fear ;
Scotland hath foisons to fill up your will
Of your mere own : all these are portable,
With other graces weigh'd.   9(

Mal. But I have none : the king-becoming graces,
As justice, verity, temperance, stableness,
Bounty, perseverance, mercy, lowliness,
Devotion, patience, courage, fortitude,
I have no relish of them, but abound
In the division of each several crime,
Acting it many ways.   Nay, had I power, I should
Pour the sweet milk of concord into hell,
Uproar the universal peace, confound
All unity on earth.

Macd.   O Scotland, Scotland !   10(

Mal. If such a one be fit to govern, speak :
    I am as I have spoken.

Macd.   Fit to govern ?
    No, not to live.   O nation miserable !
    With an untitled tyrant, bloody-scepter'd,
    When shalt thou see thy wholesome days again,
    Since that the truest issue of thy throne
    By his own interdiction stands accurs'd,
    And does blaspheme his breed ?   Thy royal father
    Was a most sainted king : the queen that bore thee,
    Oftener upon her knees than on her feet,   110
    Died every day she liv'd.   Fare thee well !
    These evils thou repeat'st upon thyself
    Have banish'd me from Scotland.   O my breast,
    Thy hope ends here !

Mal.   Macduff, this noble passion,
    Child of integrity, hath from my soul
    Wip'd the black scruples, reconcil'd my thoughts
    To thy good truth and honour.   Devilish Macbeth,
    By many of these trains, hath sought to win me
    Into his power ; and modest wisdom plucks me
    From over-credulous haste : but God above   120
    Deal between thee and me ! for even now
    I put myself to thy direction, and
    Unspeak mine own detraction ; here abjure

The taints and blames I laid upon myself,
For strangers to my nature.   I am yet
Unknown to woman, never was forsworn,
Scarcely have coveted what was mine own,
At no time broke my faith, would not betray
The devil to his fellow, and delight
No less in truth than life : my first false speaking   130
Was this upon myself : what I am truly,
Is thine and my poor country's to command :
Whither indeed, before thy here-approach,
Old Siward, with ten thousand warlike men,
Already at a point, was setting forth.
Now we 'll together, and the chance of goodness   †
Be like our warranted quarrel !   Why are you silent ?
Macd. Such welcome and unwelcome things at once
   'Tis hard to reconcile.

                    Enter a Doctor

Mal. Well, more anon. Comes the king forth, I pray you ?   140
Doc. Ay, sir ; there are a crew of wretched souls
   That stay his cure : their malady convinces
   The great assay of art ; but at his touch,
   Such sanctity hath heaven given his hand,
   They presently amend.
Mal.   I thank you, doctor.   *Exit Doctor*
Macd. What 's the disease he means ?

Mal.   'Tis call'd the evil :
A most miraculous work in this good king,
Which often, since my here-remain in England,
I have seen him do.   How he solicits heaven
Himself best knows : but strangely-visited people,   150
All swoln and ulcerous, pitiful to the eye,
The mere despair of surgery, he cures,
Hanging a golden stamp about their necks,
Put on with holy prayers, and 'tis spoken
To the succeeding royalty he leaves
The healing benediction.   With this strange virtue
He hath a heavenly gift of prophecy,
And sundry blessings hang about his throne
That speak him full of grace.

Enter Ross

Macd.   See, who comes here ?
Mal. My countryman ; but yet I know him not.   160
Macd. My ever gentle cousin, welcome hither.
Mal. I know him now : good God, betimes remove
The means that makes us strangers !
Ross.   Sir, amen.
Macd. Stands Scotland where it did ?
Ross.   Alas, poor country !
Almost afraid to know itself !   It cannot
Be call'd our mother, but our grave : where nothing,

But who knows nothing, is once seen to smile ;
Where sighs, and groans, and shrieks that rend the air,
Are made, not mark'd ; where violent sorrow seems
A modern ecstasy : the dead man's knell   †
Is there scarce ask'd for who, and good men's lives   17)
Expire before the flowers in their caps,
Dying or ere they sicken.

Macd.   O, relation
Too nice, and yet too true !

Mal.   What 's the newest grief ?

Ross. That of an hour's age doth hiss the speaker ;
Each minute teems a new one.

Macd.   How does my wife ?

Ross. Why, well.

Macd.   And all my children ?

Ross.   Well too.

Macd. The tyrant has not batter'd at their peace ?

Ross. No, they were well at peace, when I did leave 'em.

Macd. Be not a niggard of your speech : how goes 't ?   18c

Ross. When I came hither to transport the tidings,
Which I have heavily borne, there ran a rumour
Of many worthy fellows that were out,
Which was to my belief witness'd the rather,
For that I saw the tyrant's power a-foot :
Now is the time of help ; your eye in Scotland

Would create soldiers, make our women fight,
To doff their dire distresses.

Mal.   Be 't their comfort
We are coming thither : gracious England hath
Lent us good Siward, and ten thousand men ;   190
An older and a better soldier none
That Christendom gives out.

Ross.   Would I could answer
This comfort with the like !   But I have words
That would be howl'd out in the desert air,
Where hearing should not latch them.

Macd.   What concern they,
The general cause, or is it a fee-grief
Due to some single breast ?

Ross.   No mind that 's honest
But in it shares some woe, though the main part
Pertains to you alone.

Macd.   If it be mine,
Keep it not from me, quickly let me have it.   200

Ross. Let not your ears despise my tongue for ever,
Which shall possess them with the heaviest sound
That ever yet they heard.

Macd.   Hum ! I guess at it.

Ross. Your castle is surpris'd ; your wife, and babes,
Savagely slaughter'd : to relate the manner

Were on the quarry of these murder'd dear
To add the death of you.

Mal.   Merciful heaven!
What, man, ne'er pull your hat upon your brows;
Give sorrow words; the grief that does not speak
Whispers the o'erfraught heart, and bids it break.   21

Macd. My children too?

Ross.   Wife, children, servants, all
That could be found.

Macd.   And I must be from thence?
My wife kill'd too?

Ross.   I have said.

Mal.   Be comforted.
Let 's make us medicines of our great revenge,
To cure this deadly grief.

Macd. He has no children.   All my pretty ones?
Did you say all?   O hell-kite!   All?
What, all my pretty chickens, and their dam
At one fell swoop?

Mal. Dispute it like a man.

Macd.   I shall do so;   22
But I must also feel it as a man:
I cannot but remember such things were,
That were most precious to me.   Did heaven look on,
And would not take their part?   Sinful Macduff,

88

They were all struck for thee ! naught that I am,
Not for their own demerits, but for mine,
Fell slaughter on their souls : heaven rest them now !

Mal. Be this the whetstone of your sword, let grief
Convert to anger : blunt not the heart, enrage it.

Macd. O, I could play the woman with mine eyes,   230
And braggart with my tongue ! But, gentle heavens,
Cut short all intermission ; front to front
Bring thou this fiend of Scotland and myself,
Within my sword's length set him, if he 'scape,
Heaven forgive him too !

Mal.   This tune goes manly.
Come, go we to the king ; our power is ready,
Our lack is nothing but our leave.   Macbeth
Is ripe for shaking, and the powers above
Put on their instruments.   Receive what cheer you
        may ;
The night is long that never finds the day.   *Exeunt* 240

Act Fifth

SCENE I

Dunsinane.   Ante-room in the castle

Enter a Doctor of Physic and a Waiting-Gentlewoman

Doc. I have two nights watch'd with you, but can perceive no truth in your report.   When was it she last walk'd ?

Gen. Since his majesty went into the field, I have seen her rise from her bed, throw her nightgown upon her, unlock her closet, take forth paper, fold it, write upon 't, read it, afterwards seal it, and again return to bed ; yet all this while in a most fast sleep.

Doc. A great perturbation in nature, to receive at once the benefit of sleep, and do the effects of watching.   In   10 this slumbery agitation, besides her walking, and other actual performances, what (at any time) have you heard her say ?

Gen. That, sir, which I will not report after her.

Doc. You may to me, and 'tis most meet you should.

Gen. Neither to you, nor any one, having no witness to confirm my speech.

Enter Lady Macbeth, with a taper

Lo you, here she comes ! This is her very guise,
and, upon my life, fast asleep. Observe her, stand
close.   20

Doc. How came she by that light ?

Gen. Why, it stood by her : she has light by her continually, 'tis her command.

Doc. You see her eyes are open.

Gen. Ay, but their sense is shut.

Doc. What is it she does now ? Look how she rubs her
hands.

Gen. It is an accustom'd action with her, to seem thus
washing her hands : I have known her continue in
this a quarter of an hour.   30

L.M. Yet here 's a spot.

Doc. Hark ! she speaks, I will set down what comes from
her, to satisfy my remembrance the more strongly.

L.M. Out damned spot ! out I say ! One : two : why
then 'tis time to do 't : hell is murky. Fie, my lord,
fie, a soldier, and afeard ? What need we fear who
knows it, when none can call our power to account ?
Yet who would have thought the old man to have
had so much blood in him ?

Doc. Do you mark that ?   40

L.M. The thane of Fife, had a wife ; where is she now ?

What, will these hands ne'er be clean? No more o'
that, my lord, no more o' that; you mar all with
this starting.

Doc. Go to, go to; you have known what you should not.

Gen. She has spoke what she should not, I am sure of that:
heaven knows what she has known.

*L.M.*Here's the smell of the blood still: all the perfumes
of Arabia will not sweeten this little hand. Oh, oh,
oh!   50

Doc. What a sigh is there! The heart is sorely charg'd.

Gen. I would not have such a heart in my bosom for the
dignity of the whole body.

Doc. Well, well, well,—

Gen. Pray God it be, sir.

Doc. This disease is beyond my practice: yet I have
known those which have walk'd in their sleep, who
have died holily in their beds.

*L.M.*Wash your hands, put on your nightgown, look not
so pale: I tell you yet again Banquo's buried; he   60
cannot come out on's grave.

Doc. Even so?

*L.M.*To bed, to bed; there's knocking at the gate:
come, come, come, come, give me your hand:
what's done, cannot be undone: to bed, to bed,
to bed.   *Exit*

Doc. Will she go now to bed?

Gen. Directly.

Doc. Foul whisperings are abroad: unnatural deeds
　　　Do breed unnatural troubles: infected minds　　70
　　　To their deaf pillows will discharge their secrets:
　　　More needs she the divine than the physician.
　　　God, God forgive us all! Look after her,
　　　Remove from her the means of all annoyance,
　　　And still keep eyes upon her. So good night:
　　　My mind she has mated and amaz'd my sight:
　　　I think, but dare not speak.

Gen.　　　　　　　　　　　Good night, good doctor.

　　　　　　　　　　　　　　　　　　　Exeunt

SCENE II

The country near Dunsinane

Drum and colours.　Enter Menteith, Caithness, Angus,
Lennox, and Soldiers

Men. The English power is near, led on by Malcolm,
　　　His uncle Siward, and the good Macduff:
　　　Revenges burn in them; for their dear causes
　　　Would to the bleeding and the grim alarm
　　　Excite the mortified man.

Ang.   Near Birnam wood
    Shall we well meet them ; that way are they coming.
Cai. Who knows if Donalbain be with his brother ?
Len. For certain, sir, he is not : I have a file
    Of all the gentry : there is Siward's son,
    And many unrough youths, that even now   10
    Protest their first of manhood.
Men.   What does the tyrant ?
Cai. Great Dunsinane he strongly fortifies :
    Some say he 's mad ; others, that lesser hate him,
    Do call it valiant fury, but, for certain,
    He cannot buckle his distemper'd cause
    Within the belt of rule.
Ang.   Now does he feel
    His secret murders sticking on his hands,
    Now minutely revolts upbraid his faith-breach ;
    Those he commands move only in command,
    Nothing in love : now does he feel his title   20
    Hang loose about him, like a giant's robe
    Upon a dwarfish thief.
Men.   Who then shall blame
    His pester'd senses to recoil, and start,
    When all that is within him does condemn
    Itself, for being there ?
Cai.   Well, march we on,

To give obedience, where 'tis truly owed :
Meet we the medicine of the sickly weal,
And with him pour we, in our country's purge,
Each drop of us.

Len.   Or so much as it needs,
To dew the sovereign flower, and drown the weeds :   30
Make we our march towards Birnam.

Exeunt, marching

SCENE III

Dunsinane.   A room in the castle
Enter Macbeth, Doctor, and Attendants

Mac. Bring me no more reports, let them fly all :
Till Birnam wood remove to Dunsinane,
I cannot taint with fear.   What 's the boy Malcolm ?
Was he not born of woman ?   The spirits that know
All mortal consequences have pronounc'd me thus :
' Fear not, Macbeth, no man that 's born of woman
Shall e'er have power upon thee.'   Then fly, false
        thanes,
And mingle with the English epicures :
The mind I sway by, and the heart I bear,
Shall never sag with doubt, nor shake with fear.   10

Enter a Servant

    The devil damn thee black, thou cream-fac'd loon !
    Where got'st thou that goose look ?

Ser. There is ten thousand—

Mac.   Geese, villain ?

Ser.   Soldiers, sir.

Mac. Go prick thy face, and over-red thy fear,
    Thou lily-liver'd boy.   What soldiers, patch ?
    Death of thy soul ! those linen cheeks of thine
    Are counsellors to fear.   What soldiers, whey-face ?

Ser. The English force, so please you.

Mac. Take thy face hence.   *Exit Servant*

              Seyton !—I am sick at heart,
    When I behold—Seyton, I say !—This push   20
    Will cheer me ever, or disseat me now.   †
    I have liv'd long enough : my way of life
    Is fall'n into the sear, the yellow leaf,
    And that which should accompany old age,
    As honour, love, obedience, troops of friends,
    I must not look to have ; but, in their stead,
    Curses, not loud but deep, mouth-honour, breath,
    Which the poor heart would fain deny, and dare not.
    Seyton !

Enter Seyton

Sey. What 's your gracious pleasure ?

Mac.   What news more ?   30

Sey. All is confirm'd, my lord, which was reported.

Mac. I 'll fight, till from my bones my flesh be hack'd.
Give me my armour.

Sey.   'Tis not needed yet.

Mac. I 'll put it on.
Send out moe horses, skirr the country round,
Hang those that talk of fear.   Give me mine armour.
How does your patient, doctor ?

Doc.   Not so sick, my lord,
As she is troubled with thick-coming fancies
That keep her from her rest.

Mac.   Cure of that.   †
Canst thou not minister to a mind diseas'd,   40
Pluck from the memory a rooted sorrow,
Raze out the written troubles of the brain,
And with some sweet oblivious antidote
Cleanse the stuff'd bosom of that perilous stuff
Which weighs upon the heart ?

Doc.   Therein the patient
Must minister to himself.

Mac. Throw physic to the dogs, I 'll none of it.
Come, put mine armour on ; give me my staff.
Seyton, send out.   Doctor, the thanes fly from me.
Come, sir, dispatch.   If thou couldst, doctor, cast   50

97

The water of my land, find her disease,
And purge it to a sound and pristine health,
I would applaud thee to the very echo,
That should applaud again.   Pull 't off, I say.
What rhubarb, senna, or what purgative drug,   †
Would scour these English hence ?   Hear'st thou of
          them ?

Doc. Ay, my good lord ; your royal preparation
Makes us hear something.

Mac.   Bring it after me.
I will not be afraid of death and bane,
Till Birnam forest come to Dunsinane.   6o

Doc. (*aside*) Were I from Dunsinane away, and clear,
Profit again should hardly draw me here.   *Exeunt*

SCENE IV

Country near Birnam wood

*Drum and colours.   Enter Malcolm, old Siward and his Son,
    Macduff, Menteith, Caithness, Angus, Lennox, Ross,
    and Soldiers, marching*

Mal. Cousins, I hope the days are near at hand
That chambers will be safe.

Men.   We doubt it nothing.

Siw. What wood is this before us ?

Men.   The wood of Birnam.

Mal. Let every soldier hew him down a bough,
And bear 't before him, thereby shall we shadow
The numbers of our host, and make discovery
Err in report of us.

Sol.   It shall be done.

Siw. We learn no other but the confident tyrant
Keeps still in Dunsinane, and will endure
Our setting down before 't.

Mal.   'Tis his main hope :   10
For where there is advantage to be given,
Both more and less have given him the revolt,
And none serve with him but constrained things
Whose hearts are absent too.

Macd.   Let our just censures
Attend the true event, and put we on
Industrious soldiership.

Siw.   The time approaches,
That will with due decision make us know
What we shall say we have, and what we owe.
Thoughts speculative their unsure hopes relate,
But certain issue strokes must arbitrate :   20
Towards which, advance the war.   *Exeunt, marching*

SCENE V

Dunsinane.   Within the castle

Enter Macbeth, Seyton, and Soldiers, with drum and colours

Mac. Hang out our banners on the outward walls ;
　　　The cry is still ' They come : ' our castle's strength
　　　Will laugh a siege to scorn : here let them lie
　　　Till famine and the ague eat them up ;
　　　Were they not forc'd with those that should be ours,
　　　We might have met them dareful, beard to beard,
　　　And beat them backward home.

　　　　　　　　　　　　A cry within of women
　　　　　　　　　　What is that noise ?

Sey. It is the cry of women, my good lord.　　　*Exit*

Mac. I have almost forgot the taste of fears :
　　　The time has been, my senses would have cool'd　　10
　　　To hear a night-shriek, and my fell of hair
　　　Would at a dismal treatise rouse, and stir
　　　As life were in 't : I have supp'd full with horrors,
　　　Direness, familiar to my slaughterous thoughts,
　　　Cannot once start me.

　　　　　　　　　　Re-enter Seyton
　　　　　　　　　　Wherefore was that cry ?

Sey. The queen, my lord, is dead.

Mac. She should have died hereafter ;
    There would have been a time for such a word.
    To-morrow, and to-morrow, and to-morrow,
    Creeps in this petty pace from day to day,   20
    To the last syllable of recorded time ;
    And all our yesterdays, have lighted fools
    The way to dusty death.   Out, out, brief candle,
    Life 's but a walking shadow, a poor player
    That struts and frets his hour upon the stage,
    And then is heard no more.   It is a tale
    Told by an idiot, full of sound and fury,
    Signifying nothing.

Enter a Messenger

    Thou com'st to use thy tongue ; thy story quickly.

Mes. Gracious my lord,   30
    I should report that which I say I saw,
    But know not how to do it.

Mac.   Well, say, sir.

Mes. As I did stand my watch upon the hill,
    I look'd toward Birnam, and anon methought
    The wood began to move.

Mac.   Liar, and slave !

Mes. Let me endure your wrath, if 't be not so :
    Within this three mile may you see it coming ;
    I say, a moving grove.

Mac.   If thou speak'st false,
 Upon the next tree shalt thou hang alive
 Till famine cling thee : if thy speech be sooth, 40
 I care not if thou dost for me as much.
 I pull in resolution, and begin   †
 To doubt the equivocation of the fiend,
 That lies like truth : ' Fear not, till Birnam wood
 Do come to Dunsinane ; ' and now a wood
 Comes toward Dunsinane.   Arm, arm, and out !
 If this which he avouches does appear,
 There is nor flying hence nor tarrying here.
 I 'gin to be a-weary of the sun,
 And wish the estate o' the world were now undone. 50
 Ring the alarum-bell !   Blow, wind, come, wrack,
 At least we 'll die with harness on our back. *Exeunt*

SCENES VI, VII, AND VIII

Dunsinane.   Before the castle

*Drum and colours.   Enter Malcolm, old Siward, Macduff,
and their Army, with boughs*

Mal. Now near enough ; your leavy screens throw down,
 And show like those you are.   You, worthy uncle,
 Shall, with my cousin, your right noble son,

Lead our first battle : worthy Macduff and we
Shall take upon 's what else remains to do,
According to our order.

iw.   Fare you well.
Do we but find the tyrant's power to-night,
Let us be beaten, if we cannot fight.

Macd. Make all our trumpets speak ; give them all breath,
Those clamorous harbingers of blood and death.   10

Exeunt
Alarums continued

Alarums.   Enter Macbeth

Mac. They have tied me to a stake, I cannot fly,
But bear-like I must fight the course.   What 's he
That was not born of woman ?   Such a one
Am I to fear, or none.

Enter young Siward

Young Si. What is thy name ?

Mac.   Thou 'lt be afraid to hear it.

Young Si. No ; though thou call'st thyself a hotter name
Than any is in hell.

Mac.   My name 's Macbeth.

Young Si. The devil himself could not pronounce a title
   More hateful to mine ear.

Mac.   No, nor more fearful.

Young Si. Thou liest, abhorred tyrant; with my sword   10
   I'll prove the lie thou speak'st.

                   They fight, and young Siward is slain

Mac.   Thou wast born of woman;
   But swords I smile at, weapons laugh to scorn,
   Brandish'd by man that's of a woman born.   *Exit*

              Alarums.   Enter Macduff

Macd. That way the noise is.   Tyrant, show thy face !
   If thou be'st slain and with no stroke of mine,
   My wife and children's ghosts will haunt me still.
   I cannot strike at wretched kerns, whose arms
   Are hir'd to bear their staves : either thou, Macbeth,
   Or else my sword with an unbatter'd edge
   I sheathe again undeeded.   There thou shouldst be ;   20
   By this great clatter, one of greatest note
   Seems bruited : let me find him, fortune,
   And more I beg not.   *Exit.   Alarums*

              Enter Malcolm and old Siward

Siw. This way, my lord, the castle's gently render'd :
   The tyrant's people on both sides do fight,
   The noble thanes do bravely in the war,
   The day almost itself professes yours,

And little is to do.

Mal.   We have met with foes
That strike beside us.

Siw.   Enter, sir, the castle.

         Exeunt. *Alarum*

Enter Macbeth

Mac. Why should I play the Roman fool, and die
On mine own sword ? whiles I see lives, the gashes
Do better upon them.

Enter Macduff

Macd.   Turn, hell-hound, turn !

Mac. Of all men else I have avoided thee :
But get thee back, my soul is too much charg'd
With blood of thine already.

Macd.   I have no words,
My voice is in my sword, thou bloodier villain
Than terms can give thee out ! *They fight*

Mac.   Thou losest labour ;
As easy mayst thou the intrenchant air
With thy keen sword impress, as make me bleed : 10

    Let fall thy blade on vulnerable crests,
    I bear a charmed life, which must not yield
    To one of woman born.

Macd.   Despair thy charm,
    And let the angel whom thou still hast serv'd
    Tell thee, Macduff was from his mother's womb
    Untimely ripp'd.

Mac. Accursed be that tongue that tells me so ;
    For it hath cow'd my better part of man !
    And be these juggling fiends no more believ'd,
    That palter with us in a double sense,   20
    That keep the word of promise to our ear,
    And break it to our hope.   I 'll not fight with thee.

Macd. Then yield thee coward,
    And live to be the show and gaze o' the time :
    We 'll have thee, as our rarer monsters are,   †
    Painted upon a pole, and underwrit,
    ' Here may you see the tyrant.'

Mac.   I will not yield
    To kiss the ground before young Malcolm's feet,
    And to be baited with the rabble's curse.
    Though Birnam wood be come to Dunsinane,   30
    And thou oppos'd, being of no woman born,
    Yet I will try the last : before my body
    I throw my warlike shield : lay on, Macduff ;

And damn'd be him that first cries ' Hold, enough ! '
                              Exeunt, fighting.   Alarums
                 Enter fighting, and Macbeth slain   †
         Retreat and flourish.   Enter, with drum and colours, Malcolm,
            old Siward, Ross, the other Thanes, and Soldiers

Mal. I would the friends we miss were safe arriv'd.

Siw. Some must go off : and yet by these I see
So great a day as this is cheaply bought.

Mal. Macduff is missing, and your noble son.

Ross. Your son, my lord, has paid a soldier's debt :
He only liv'd but till he was a man,   40
The which no sooner had his prowess confirm'd
In the unshrinking station where he fought,
But like a man he died.

Siw.   Then he is dead ?

Ross. Ay, and brought off the field : your cause of sorrow
Must not be measur'd by his worth, for then
It hath no end.

Siw.   Had he his hurts before ?

Ross. Ay, on the front.

Siw.   Why then, God's soldier be he !
Had I as many sons as I have hairs,
I would not wish them to a fairer death :
And so his knell is knoll'd.

Mal.   He 's worth more sorrow,   50

And that I 'll spend for him.

Siw.   He 's worth no more,
They say he parted well, and paid his score :
And so God be with him ! Here comes newer
comfort.

Re-enter Macduff, with Macbeth's head

Macd. Hail, king ! for so thou art : behold where stands
The usurper's cursed head : the time is free :
I see thee compass'd with thy kingdom's pearl,
That speak my salutation in their minds ;
Whose voices I desire aloud with mine :
Hail, King of Scotland !

All.   Hail, King of Scotland !

Flourish

Mal. We shall not spend a large expense of time
Before we reckon with your several loves,
And make us even with you. My thanes and kins-
men,
Henceforth be earls, the first that ever Scotland
In such an honour nam'd. What 's more to do,
Which would be planted newly with the time,
As calling home our exil'd friends abroad,
That fled the snares of watchful tyranny,
Producing forth the cruel ministers
Of this dead butcher, and his fiend-like queen,

Who (as 'tis thought) by self and violent hands   70
Took off her life ; this, and what needful else
That calls upon us, by the grace of Grace
We will perform in measure, time and place :
So thanks to all at once, and to each one,
Whom we invite to see us crown'd at Scone.

Flourish.   Exeunt

Notes

I. ii. 21. *Which ne'er shook hands . . .*; the only antecedent for *which* that will make sense is *Macbeth*. This is awkward and suggests an unjoined cut.

I. iii. 15. *ports they blow*; emendations such as *points* or *orts* (airts) are unnecessary if we understand *blow* to mean ' blow to.'

I. iii. 32. *weird*; F reads *weyward*, and so (or sometimes *weyard*) later: but it can hardly be anything but a variant spelling of *weird*, perhaps influenced by the O.E. ' wyrd '=' fate.'

I. iii. 97-98. *hail Came post*; Rowe's usually accepted emendation of F's *tale Can post*. It gives good enough sense, except that one would rather have expected *post* on *post*, but it is not easy to see how the corruption arose, and I rather suspect a cut.

I. iii. 131, 134. *ill? . . . good?*; F's punctuation is retained.

I. iv. 44. *The rest is labour . . .*; this must mean 'that leisure which is not used for you is no rest, but toil,' but it is an awkward phrase.

I. vii. 45. *the poor cat i' the adage*; " The cate would eate fyshe, and would not wet her feete."

I. vii. 60. *We fail?* So F. Some commentators would read an exclamation mark (for which the mark of interrogation is commonly printed in Elizabethan texts) and make the phrase mean ' Very good, if we fail, we fail.'

II. i. 55. *Tarquin*; Tarquinius Superbus of Rome, who ravished Lucrece, wife of Collatine.

II. ii. 63. *making the green one red*; this is the accepted modern reading and gives the more vigorous sense. But one should note that the Elizabethan punctuation for that would probably be *making the green, one red*, whereas F reads *making the green one, red*.

110

II. iii. 9. *equivocator*; almost certainly an allusion to the trial of the Jesuit Garnet in 1606.

III. i. 130. *Acquaint you . . .*; of the many explanations I think Herford's the best, 'tell you the right moment as determined by exact inspection.'

III. ii. 13. *scotch'd*; Theobald's emendation of F's *scorch'd*: *t* and *r* were so nearly alike in ordinary Elizabethan type that there was always a danger of foul case. I leave the emendation, since it is quite probable, and hallowed by familiarity, but it was not needed, since *scorch* means 'to cut.'

III. ii. 32. *Unsafe the while . . .*; if we are to extract a meaning from this it must be by taking the words 'absolutely'; either 'the interval is unsafe, inasmuch as . . .,' or 'the interval is unsafe during which.' But the incomplete line is suspicious and there is probably corruption.

III. iii. (S.D.). *Enter three Murderers*; this third murderer is mysterious. It has been conjectured that he is Macbeth himself, which would no doubt be effective; but then he ought to know later that Fleance escaped. He is probably merely a spy of Macbeth's, as the Second Murderer's speech implies.

III. iv. 33. *You do not give . . . welcome*; the punctuation is given as in F. Most editions give a comma after *making* and no stop after *given*, with the interpretation 'the feast is no free gift in the course of which the entertainer does not often declare that it is given with welcome.' But the F reading is at least possible, and has the advantage that it gives a contrast between *sold* and *given* which the other wholly misses: 'the feast is no free gift which is not, in the course of it, guaranteed (*i.e.* as a free feast); but it *is* a free gift when welcome is expressed at it.' The real difficulty is the word 'sold,' since there seems to be no proper sense in which a feast is 'sold.'

If we were to emend to *cold* the modern punctuation would give good sense, but the emendation is impossible to justify.

III. iv. 128-30. The silence of most commentators indicates that they find this passage lucid—or incomprehensible. But it surely is not lucid at all. To begin with, Lady Macbeth has made no comment at all about Macduff, so that the straightforward interpretation of Macbeth's remark is out of court. He must mean either ' what do you make of the fact that Macduff . . .' (*i.e.* ' what do you know about that? '), or, possibly, ' what do you think? I Macduff . . .?' Lady Macbeth's rejoinder is plain common sense But Macbeth's answer only adds to the puzzle, since, unless he had sent, Macduff cannot in any proper sense be said to have ' denied ' anything, since he had no bidding to deny. One wonders whether Macbeth's opening means rather ' Do you think that Macduff *will* deny . . .?', and that he continues 'I hear reports of his disaffection and I will send to test it.'

IV. i. 97. *Rebellious dead*; so F. Usually emended to ' Rebellion' head.' But I think Macbeth is thinking rather of the unquiet ghost of Banquo.

IV. ii. 22. *Each way, and move*; so F. But there is much to be said for the emendation *Each way, and none.*

IV. ii. 83 (S.D.). This is the usual stage-direction. But F gives *Exit crying Murther*, as though the boy were not killed outright but had enough life left to flee. The murderers then presumably turn on Lady Macduff.

IV. iii. 15. *discern*; Theobald's emendation *deserve* makes sense which is more than can be said of *discern*, and would be acceptable if it were not that the whole passage looks as though there were some dislocation.

IV. iii. 136 *Be like*; this passage is thoroughly obscure. There seems no reason why the *chance of goodness* (whatever that means) should resemble a quarrel, however well warranted. If one could extract any satisfactory meaning from *Belike* as a verb, something might be made of it, but there is no feasible sense recognised. Cuningham, to whom valour is more often than not the better part of discretion, would emend to *grace of goodness Betide*, which may indeed be what Shakespeare wrote, since nothing is beyond an Elizabethan compositor, but can hardly be justified by probabilities.

IV. iii. 170. *the dead man's knell . . .*; I think that this means 'death is so frequent that no one asks for whom the bell is tolling'; but it may mean 'the bell does not toll for anyone' (an archaic indefinite use of *who*).

V. iii. 21. *cheer . . . disseat*; F reads *cheere . . . dis-eate*. There is clearly (if *disseat* is right) a pun on *chair* ('to enthrone in honour'), and we should perhaps read *chair*.

V. iii. 39. *Cure of that*; the later Ff and modern editors read *Cure her of that*. But I feel that though there is probably an omission the command is awkward before the following question, and also that Macbeth's remark is more general than particular; *i.e.* that it would be better represented by, for example, *No cure of that?*

V. iii. 55. *senna*; F reads *Cyme*, which is usually taken to be a misreading of some such form (otherwise unknown) as *Cynne*: but the old spelling was *sena*, and one can feel no confidence in the reading.

V. v. 42. *pull in resolution*; usually taken to mean 'check my resolution,' *pull in* being taken together: but this seems as bad in rhythm as in sense: one wants an intransitive verb (*e.g. pule*) so that *in resolution* can be taken together.

V. viii. 25. *as our rarer monsters . . .*; *i.e.* as a notice of a rarity is painted (on a board or cloth) and hung on a pole at a fair.

V. viii. 34 (S.D.). *Enter fighting, and Macbeth slain*; so F. It is usually omitted by modern editions, on the ground that it will not square with Macduff's later entry with Macbeth's head. But the exit of the two, the empty stage, and their re-entry on to it, has a certain effectiveness, and if Macbeth is 'slain,' or at any rate receives what is clearly his fatal wound, just as they go off, it is not unworkable.

Glossary

MANY words and phrases in Shakespeare require glossing, not because they are in themselves unfamiliar, but for the opposite reason, that Shakespeare uses in their Elizabethan and unfamiliar sense a large number of words which seem so familiar that there is no incentive to look for them in the glossary. It is hoped that a glossary arranged as below will make it easy to see at a glance what words and phrases in any particular scene require elucidation. A number of phrases are glossed by what seems to be, in their context, the modern equivalent rather than by lexicographical glosses on the words which compose them.

Act First

SCENE I

line
8 GRAYMALKIN, (*prop.* grey cat, *here*) name of a fiend

line
9 PADDOCK, (*prop.* toad, *here probably also*) name of a fiend

SCENE II

13 OF, with
KERNS AND GALLOWGLASSES, Irish soldiers
19 MINION, darling
22 NAVE, navel
CHOPS, jaws
37 CRACKS, charges

40 MEMORIZE, make memorable
54 BELLONA, goddess of war
LAPP'D IN PROOF, fully armed
62 INCH, islet
65 BOSOM INTEREST, intimate confidence

SCENE III

6 AROINT, avaunt!
RUMP-FED, fed on scraps

6 RONYON, term of abuse
22 SE'NNIGHTS, weeks (seven nights)

Act I Sc. iii—*continued*

line		line	
23	PEAK, grow thin	56	ROYAL HOPE, hope of kingship
33	POSTERS, scourers	76	OWE, have
53	FANTASTICAL, illusory	112	LINE, support
56	HAVING, estate	139	FANTASTICAL, imagined

SCENE IV

10	OW'D, possessed	41	SIGNS OF NOBLENESS, insignia of nobility
11	CARELESS, unvalued		
19	PROPORTION, adequate return		

SCENE V

49	SIGHTLESS SUBSTANCES, invisible existences	72	FAVOUR, expression

SCENE VI

6	JUTTY, projecting corner	22	PURVEYOR, 'courier'

SCENE VII

7	JUMP, 'chance'	67	RECEIPT, seat
23	SIGHTLESS, invisible	68	LIMBEC, alembic
65	CONVINCE, subdue	72	SPONGY, sodden
67	A FUME, *i.e.* 'fumed,' drugged	73	QUELL, murder

Act Second

SCENE I

14	OFFICES, kitchen, etc. (*or* (?) 'staff')	46	DUDGEON, hilt
			GOUTS, drops
16	SHUT UP, wrapped in	48	INFORMS, conjures up shapes
28	FRANCHIS'D, free	52	HECAT, goddess of night (and so of witchcraft)
36	SENSIBLE, apprehensible		

SCENE II

SCENE III

SCENE IV

Act Third

SCENE I

MACBETH

SCENE II

line
- 13 SCOTCH'D, cut
- 16 DISJOINT, come to pieces
  SUFFER, perish
- 22 RESTLESS ECSTASY, unbalanced
  excitement

line
- 38 COPY, *either* pattern, *or* tenure
  (copy-hold)
- 42 SHARD, (*prop.* wing case, *and so*)
  wing
- 46 SEELING, closing the eyes (*prop.*
  of a hawk)

SCENE III

- 10 WITHIN THE NOTE OF EXPECTA-
  TION, on the list of expected
  guests

SCENE IV

- 1 DEGREES, precedence
- 19 THE NONPAREIL, unequalled
- 23 GENERAL, unconfined
  CASING, *i.e.* surrounding every-
  thing
- 24 CRIBB'D, cramped
- 25 SAUCY, intrusive
- 29 WORM, snake
- 40 ROOF'D, under the roof
- 63 FLAWS, outbursts

- 66 AUTHORIZ'D, passed down
- 95 SPECULATION, sight *or* intelligence
- 110 ADMIR'D, wondered at
- 124 AUGURES, auguries
  UNDERSTOOD RELATIONS, properly
  interpreted phenomena
- 125 MAGGOT-PIES, magpies
  CHOUGHS, jackdaws
  BROUGHT FORTH, revealed

SCENE VI

- 25 HOLDS, withholds
- 40 WITH, having received an
  answer

- 41 CLOUDY, surly

Act Fourth

SCENE I

ne		*line*	
17	HOWLET, owlet	53	YESTY, frothy
23	MUMMY, a medicinal preparation (liquid or dry) from mummies	59	GERMINS, seeds
		65	NINE FARROW, litter of nine
	GULF, belly	74	HARP'D, guessed
24	RAVIN'D, (?) glutted	84	TAKE A BOND OF, enter into a bond with
32	SLAB, semi-solid	88	ROUND, crown
33	CHAUDRON, innards		

SCENE II

34	LIME, bird-lime	63	IN YOUR STATE OF HONOUR I AM PERFECT, ' I know you are Lady Macduff '
35	GIN, trap	81	SHAG-EAR'D, shaggy-eared

SCENE III

19	RECOIL, deny its nature	119	MODEST, cool
29	JEALOUSIES, suspicions	135	AT A POINT, in readiness
34	AFFEER'D, confirmed	142	CONVINCES, resists
55	CONFINELESS, limitless	143	ART, skill
67	TOP, surpass	170	MODERN ECSTASY, commonplace emotion
68	LUXURIOUS, lustful		
71	CONVEY, manage secretly	174	NICE, detailed
88	FOISONS, plenty	196	FEE-GRIEF, grief with particular owner
89	PORTABLE, bearable		
18	TRAINS, baits	210	O'ERFRAUGHT, overladen

Act Fifth

SCENE I

line

5 NIGHTGOWN, dressing-gown
10 WATCHING, waking
20 CLOSE, aside
51 CHARG'D, burdened

line

52, 53 FOR THE DIGNITY OF THE WHOLE BODY, *i.e.* not ever to be Lady Macbeth
73 ANNOYANCE, injury
75 MATED, confounded

SCENE II

3 DEAR, near to the heart
5 MORTIFIED, moribund
10 UNROUGH, unbearded

15 DISTEMPER'D, out of hand
27 WEAL, commonwealth

SCENE III

3 TAINT, become infected
8 EPICURES, sybarites
15 PATCH, fellow
20 PUSH, crisis

35 MOE, more (*Eliz. plur.*)
SKIRR, scour
43 OBLIVIOUS, bringing oblivion

SCENE V

11 FELL OF HAIR, scalp
12 DISMAL TREATISE, tale of horror

40 CLING, wither
52 HARNESS, armour

SCENE VII

17 KERNS, poorly armed soldiers

24 RENDER'D, surrendered

SCENE VIII

1 ROMAN FOOL, *e.g.* Brutus or Antony
9 INTRENCHANT, invulnerable

20 PALTER, juggle
68 PRODUCING FORTH, bringing to justice